on the outside looking indian

on the outside looking indian

HOW MY
SECOND CHILDHOOD
CHANGED MY LIFE

Rupinder Gill

RIVERHEAD BOOKS
New York

RIVERHEAD BOOKS
Published by the Penguin Group
Penguin Group (USA) Inc.
375 Hudson Street, New York, New York 10014, USA
Penguin Group (Canada), 90 Eglinton Avenue East, Suite 700, Toronto, Ontario M4P 2Y3, Canada (a division of Pearson Penguin Canada Inc.) • Penguin Books Ltd., 80 Strand, London WC2R 0RL, England • Penguin Group Ireland, 25 St. Stephen's Green, Dublin 2, Ireland (a division of Penguin Books Ltd.) • Penguin Group (Australia), 250 Camberwell Road, Camberwell, Victoria 3124, Australia (a division of Pearson Australia Group Pty. Ltd.) • Penguin Books India Pvt. Ltd., 11 Community Centre, Panchsheel Park, New Delhi—110 017, India • Penguin Group (NZ), 67 Apollo Drive, Rosedale, Auckland 0632, New Zealand (a division of Pearson New Zealand Ltd.) • Penguin Books (South Africa) (Pty.) Ltd., 24 Sturdee Avenue, Rosebank, Johannesburg 2196, South Africa

Penguin Books Ltd., Registered Offices: 80 Strand, London WC2R 0RL, England

Cover design by Jaya Micelli
Book design by Tiffany Estreicher

Originally published in Canada by McClelland & Stewart: March 2011
First Riverhead trade paperback edition: May 2012
Riverhead trade paperback ISBN: 978-1-59448-577-0

Library of Congress Cataloging-in-Publication Data

Gill, Rupinder, date.
On the outside looking Indian : how my second childhood changed my life / Rupinder Gill.—1st Riverhead trade pbk. ed.
p. cm.
Originally published: Toronto : McClelland & Stewart, c2011.
ISBN 978-1-59448-577-0
1. Gill, Rupinder. 2. Women, East Indian—Canada–Biography. 3. East Indians—Canada—Biography. 4. East Indians—Canada—Social life and customs. I. Title.
CT310.G435A3 2012
971.00491'4—dc23
2012001308

PRINTED IN THE UNITED STATES OF AMERICA

10 9 8 7 6 5 4 3 2 1

Penguin is committed to publishing works of quality and integrity.
In that spirit, we are proud to offer this book to our readers;
however, the story, the experiences, and the words are the author's alone.

For my parents and my siblings,
who, in letting me tell my story, let me tell theirs too.

→ INTRODUCTION ←

girls gone mild

There is a phenomenon in Amish culture called "Rumspringa," where Amish adolescents are permitted to break free from their modest and traditional lifestyles and indulge in normally taboo activities. They dress how they want, go out if and when they please, smoke, drink, and party like it's 1899. At the end of their Springa Break, they decide whether they will maintain their new lifestyles or return and join the Amish Church.

In Indian adolescence, you never break free of the rules. You cook, clean, babysit, clean, get good grades, clean, be silent, clean, and don't challenge your parents in any way, especially while cleaning. This was my life. I grew up in a town whiter than snow, about an hour outside of Toronto. Like most children of immigrants, I was raised by the rules of one culture and looked longingly at those living a distinctly different way.

I didn't have the time for a continent-wide census, but from what I know, this is how the typical North American kid spends its summer vacations growing up:

July: Summer camp, family trip, or cottage. Activities include swimming, canoeing, traveling, laughter, horseplay, tomfoolery, and general merriment. Mother makes glazed hams while father reads Russian classics and smokes a pipe. Kids dance around maypoles.

August: Return home and play with friends, have sleepovers, take weekend trips, and shop for fabulous new back-to-school clothes while dreading the inevitable return to academia.

Here is how I spent my summer vacations growing up:

July: TV room. Activities include hanging out with my sisters and watching anything and everything on television, including *Welcome Back, Kotter; Who's the Boss?; 227;* and various other programs offering canned laughter and some much-needed escapism. Brief breaks for housecleaning and being nagged for not cleaning enough.

August: Basement TV room (much cooler). Count down the return to school/find blank VHS tapes on which to tape *Days of Our Lives* (dying to know if Patch and Kayla will get together!). Fight with parents about their annual two-shirts, two-pants, back-to-school shopping policy. Pray that sideburns spontaneously fall off by Labor Day.

If an Indian version of a Rumspringa existed, a "Ram-Singha" of sorts, I would bet my last rupee that at the end of it, only one out of every hundred kids would return to their traditional Indian upbringings. The rest of us would be hanging at the mall in acid-washed jeans, schooling the younger members of the group on how to undo their parental shackles and integrate into Western society. Sessions would be set up for courses like "You Are Not Your Cousin Ravi: How to Function in a Culture That Doesn't Compare You Against Everybody Else's Kids" and "Less Is More: A Workshop in Applying Men's Musk Oil Cologne."

Unfortunately no such program existed during my adolescence, so my parents raised us by the standard rules of northern Punjab nunneries. I don't wholly blame my parents for my lackluster childhood. Having been to India, I am aware that the majority of kids there don't spend their summers singing around campfires or learning to play the flute. From a young age, you are expected to make a contribution to the house, not simply hang your favorite cartoon posters up in it.

Whenever we complained, my parents liked to remind us that they didn't grow up like Richie and Joannie Cunningham either. "When I was a kid, we made toys out of mud," my dad once said. This was the Indian equivalent of the walking-two-miles-to-school tale that white parents used as their trump card. According to my dad, they would fashion mud cars, mud guns, or mud animals and pray it didn't rain before they finished their game of cops and robbers.

With their own childhoods so limited, I understood why they didn't see value in the things we were missing out on. But the fact that *they* seemed to miss was that they weren't living in India anymore.

They tried desperately to hold on to their culture. For years, the only friends they had were fellow Indians. I took the opposite approach. Growing up, I had friends but I didn't have a single Indian friend. This was partially due to the fact that there were only a few other Indians in our primary school but also because I was not interested in all things Indian. I grew bored of Bollywood films, didn't listen to Indian music, and ate cereal for dinner so I didn't have to eat *saag*. I viewed the fact that I was Indian as the reason I lived my life hanging out in my basement. It was the reason I couldn't go to dances, go to movies past 5 P.M., take singing lessons, or be friends with boys, so I wasn't really interested in embracing any more of the culture than I was required.

In high school, there were a few other Indian kids at my school, who all hung out together, but I never made it into the fellowship. I didn't know the first thing about the latest and greatest Bhangra tracks and couldn't roll a Samosa crust to save my life.

That left my only source of comparison to be with my white friends, and it seemed fairly clear that we had very different lives. For starters, they had two distinctive eyebrows while I had one hibernating slug atop my eyes. Their parents knew the names of their kids' friends and welcomed them into their homes. But more importantly, they had freedom. My version of freedom, at least. They had the luxury of indulging their interests. They went to "lessons" and "hung out" on weekends. They went on family trips and actually had stories to tell in September when the teacher asked us what we did on our summer vacations.

I wanted that and didn't understand why I couldn't have it. Suffice it to say, my parents were strict. I was rarely allowed to go out. I wasn't allowed to take lessons, or talk on the phone with boys, or for extended periods with girls. I was discouraged from being too involved in extracurricular activities. I was expected to have good grades, although cleaning and taking care of the needs of houseguests trumped homework. I was not allowed to attend sleepovers nor were my friends ever invited into our home. I was, however, permitted to watch hours upon hours of television because television kept us quiet and indoors. Unfortunately for my parents, it just further exposed us to lives that other kids were leading. Those kids had even cooler clothes and adventures than the real kids I knew, pushing my feelings of unjustness into feelings of anger. I wanted to punch the TV every time those smug Cosby kids were on it.

One sunny August weekend not too long ago, my high school friends and I went up to our friend Jessie's cottage. We were celebrating her and our friend Johanna's upcoming weddings. As I sat on the dock and watched my friends swim in a crystal-clear lake, I felt envious. It was not for their marriages, but for their ability to swim. I couldn't swim. I had spent my whole life sitting on pool decks, standing in shallow ends, or simply avoiding the situation altogether. If we'd been at an ice-skating rink instead of a lake, I wouldn't have been able to participate there either. Ditto for skiing, tennis, gymnastics, camping, swapping stories about family vacations, or reminiscing about teenage love. I didn't have camp friends or photos of me dressed as a bumblebee in my dance classes. Never having been on a team, I didn't have a rusty Little League trophy.

I had always joked about how boring and uneventful my childhood had been. That day, the reality of it truly hit me. I had lost hundreds of hours of my childhood and missed countless experiences as I sat in front of that television. It may have been that I had just turned thirty, an age that makes you evaluate your life, whether you want to or not. It may also have been that I was surrounded by the very friends I watched have the childhood experiences I wanted.

For years I believed that childhood experiences (or the lack thereof) were strictly once in a lifetime. I always thought, When I have my own kids, they'll do all of the things I never did. But that day, as I contemplated risking death for a few minutes of feeling the water lap around me, I didn't care about those hypothetical future kids. Those jerks weren't going to put me through eighteen hours of labor *and* be rewarded for it with clarinet lessons. Out of a childhood lived in a fun-proof cave had grown an adult who didn't take chances, who didn't boldly go anywhere, and who was, well, quite bored with my routine-filled life. I needed to experience what I missed for myself, or I would forever live a life of sitting on the sidelines.

When I got back to the city, I vowed I would finally learn to swim. As I researched lessons in my neighborhood, I started to get excited at the thought of diving into a pool on a hot day, like they always do in diet soda commercials. I also started thinking about all of the other lost experiences of youth. There were so many other things I wished I had done as a kid, so whenever I would think of a new one, I would write it down. Soon I became overly ambitious. As summer gave way to the cool of fall, and the fall turned to the bitter cold of winter, my list grew. I culled out some items because I really didn't think it was *that* important that I learned to tie-dye my own scrunchies, and soon I had created a workable list of goals.

It wasn't until January that I started to take action on the list. It was a new year, I was thirty, and it felt like the perfect time for a new start. The items on the list were some of the missing links between the life I had and the one I wanted. A few were life skills, some were just desires, but all of them were important enough that I felt they warranted pursuing. There were a million more items I could have added, but I started by setting five concrete goals to tackle. The list read as follows, in no particular order:

1. LEARN TO SWIM. Indians don't swim. They don't have cottages, they don't go on cruises, and they are rarely seen basking in the sun at the beach. Indian girls especially don't swim because only a fool would think that learning a lifesaving skill was more important than keeping your body hidden forever. No doubt the women's Indian swimming team practices in full snowsuits with matching glittery bracelets. This was a life skill I just assumed I would never have and it was time to change that thinking.

2. TAKE LESSONS. Oh, how I wanted to take lessons when I was a kid. How I wanted to hate my piano teacher and do dance routines in the junior high talent show like all of the other girls. What I would have given to say, "I can't, I have karate," or "No thanks, I have to get to

gymnastics," instead of "I have to go! It's my night to clean the stove!"

3. VISIT DISNEY WORLD. Yes, I know, not every kid visited Disney World, but I always dreamed of it. Like many children with boring home lives, my fantasy life was incredibly vivid and involved many imaginary characters from the Disney catalog, children's stories, and various nonsensical cartoons. We would record Disney specials from TV onto VHS tapes and watch them over and over, fast-forwarding through the commercials for Hypercolor shirts and MiniPops.

4. GO TO CAMP. I longed to sleep on a flea-bitten mattress on a wooden plank, swim among leeches, and sing "Kumbaya" while roasting s'mores to perfection. In the seventh grade, the junior high school offered an end-of-the-year camp trip. Two weeks before the deposit was due, I took the permission slip to my dad and offered him a sales pitch straight out of *Glengarry Glen Ross*. "Forget it," he told me. I was always given the suggestion to "forget" whatever I wanted. If only he could have forgotten to say no just once. As a desperate measure, I went to my mom, who simply asked what my father had said. Two days before the application was due, I grew frantic. All of my classmates had already committed and the only people outstanding were ethnic girls and suspected bed wetters. Knowing that both of my parents would leave by 6:30 A.M. for their jobs, I woke up at six and went downstairs for one last effort. At least they were considerate enough to yell no in less

than a minute, allowing me to go back to bed and get another hour of sleep before school.

5. HAVE A PET. I have wanted a dog my whole life. All of my sisters have. We would take books out of the library on dog breeds, buy dog magazines, cut pictures of cute pups out of them, and dream of the day that our parents' tundra hearts would melt. My mom always had the same response: "I have enough animals in this house already!" It was a killer joke in the Indian mothers' circle. But I was out of her house now, and what would make my house a home more than a furry foot warmer to sit with me while I watched *Seinfeld* reruns?

I typed out my list, the same way I had typed out hundreds of lists before it. And like every list I had ever made, I wondered how I was going to really achieve any of it.

"Set one new New Year's resolution for each year until you're done," my friend Madeleine suggested.

"You know how that goes," I said. Madeleine and I met in college and created a deep friendship based on a mutual love of eating, complaining about our weight, and cracking jokes nobody else found amusing. Each year we swapped lists of New Year's resolutions that we abandoned like clockwork by January 15.

In fact, I don't think I ever finished one of my New Year's resolutions in my whole life. I never learned to do the Worm (1988), alphabetized my VHS movie tapes (1994), read every book on the *New York Times* fiction list (1998), or lost ten pounds (2001, 2002, 2003, 2004, 2005, 2006).

If I tried to do one item on the list each year, I'd have one foot in a ballet shoe and the other in the grave by the time I got around to them all. There was only one logical solution I could think of: I would have to do them all at once.

It was a bit of a goal-setting stretch for someone who had not achieved the vast majority of goals she set for herself, but if I pulled it off, perhaps I could finally stop looking at the past and move gracefully into the future. Thirty seemed as good an age as any to finish off my youth. And if I had time left at the end, maybe I would learn to do the Worm.

part one

→ ONE ←

the facts of no life

When I was twelve, my little brother, Sumeet, was born, changing our family forever. I recall exactly how I got the news. I was shopping at Kmart with my mom when she picked up a stuffed animal and put it into the shopping cart. "Who's that for?" I asked.

"The baby," she said in English, which she rarely spoke to us back then.

"Whose baby?" I said. This was a fair question because Indian women were notoriously coy about their pregnancies. Even as their stomachs are near the bursting point, they deny it. "No, no." They giggle innocently as the baby crowns and reaches out a tiny hand. "I don't know what you're talking about."

I prodded my mom again. "Whose baby?" I repeated,

throwing a bag of licorice into the shopping cart while her head was turned.

"Mine," she said, with such nonchalance that I thought she was kidding. But three months later, we confirmed that the fifth time was a charm: after four girls, it was finally a boy. The birth of a boy in an Indian home could most closely be compared to winning the largest lottery in the world and then accidentally creating an immortality potion from a mixture of 7-Eleven Slurpee flavors.

He definitely lightened the mood in our house while simultaneously adding another dimension of chores my sisters and I thought were long over. We had a four-person relay approach to changing diapers and incorporated watching over him with our daily activities. I would sit him on the handlebars of the stationary bike while I exercised in the basement and searched for all of the tools he needed to create a fort while I talked through math problems on the phone with classmates.

Having a brother also let me witness firsthand the childhood I had wanted for my own. When Sumeet started swimming lessons, we would take him to the pool each week, watching from the stands. He would jump in, run across the deck, and, every so often, wave at us. During his tennis lessons one particularly sweltering August, we sat in the grass and watched him chase tennis balls around the court. At soccer, we hovered on the sidelines with the Popsicles for the team's break. He went to birthday parties and had adorable clothing and my sisters and I were so happy about it because he was a sweet little boy whose only fault was a love for turning the garden hose on our unsuspecting grandmother.

Still, no matter how much an Indian girl loves her brother, there are certain instances in her life where she is acutely aware of the differences between their upbringings. Happy as we were that Sumeet had the opportunity to take the lessons, attend the class trips we were denied, and get every toy and piece of clothing he pointed his finger at, it didn't make us desire that same consideration any less.

"Don't jealous my son!" my mom would say when we pointed out the inequity of asking us to leave our math homework to walk beside him as he rode his motorized jeep around the neighborhood. The thing is, we didn't really jealous her son. In fact, we spoiled him almost as much as my parents did because we didn't want him to feel the way we had, like we were lesser than the other kids.

When I was in the third grade, I would go home for lunch every single day. Our house was just a ten-minute walk from the school, and one hot June day, after a lunch of grandma-grilled *parathas* and a *Scooby-Doo* episode, I headed back out to school. As I walked down a shrub-lined path, I saw one of the school bullies approaching. I didn't even know his name but I certainly knew his reputation. If this was *Freaks and Geeks,* he would shove me into the bushes, and when I went to his house with my dorky best friend Bill to retaliate with a bag of flaming dog crap, I would see he lived in a dilapidated trailer where he was forced to perform in the family's knife-throwing circus act. I would pity him and we would bond over a love of sci-fi films, becoming lifelong friends. But in real life, the kid walking toward me was likely just a jerk with no endearing backstory and I knew I was about to suffer a humiliation of sorts. I slowed down so he would end up walking ahead of me. I halted my steps, looking through my book bag as if I was searching for something. I wanted to blend into the scenery, but my shorts set had pictures of bright green cacti on it, shrubbery that wasn't native to small-town Canada. The bully, who was picking up stones and throwing them at robins flying by, spotted me. I continued slowly down the path, hoping some bodybuilding Good Samaritans would soon jog by, but no such reprieve appeared. He held a stone in his hand and waited. Trying not to make eye contact, I took one step closer to him and readied myself for the inevitable. But instead of tripping or chasing me, as I expected, he launched a verbal attack that struck even harder.

"Nice outfit," he snickered. "Four dollars at BiWay."

Although I wanted to cry, I kept my face neutral, as if I wasn't aware the comment was directed at me. The week earlier I had begged my mom not to buy me that outfit from that store. BiWay was a chain bargain store in which a school-age kid did not want to be caught dead. If a child actress wore a BiWay dress to the Emmys and was asked, "Who are you wearing?" by a grinning Mary Hart, the girl would likely hurdle the barrier to the street and flag down the nearest taxi to the airport.

You see, the only thing worse than being seen in BiWay was being identified as being dressed in BiWay. The bully carried on toward school laughing, knowing he had achieved his goal of pointing out the fact that I must be poor. At the time I was too humiliated to realize that the only way he could have known my outfit was from BiWay was if he shopped there, too.

My family wasn't poor but the area in which we lived was

unquestionably lower middle class. My parents didn't believe that kids needed brand-name clothes, so when it came time for back-to-school shopping, we would head to the mall, where I would walk at least ten feet in front of my family, not wanting to be seen with them. I tried to lead them past BiWay, but I always knew they were going to turn. I kept dreaming that they would walk right past it and my mother would say, "This year, let's get everything at Benetton!" But that was never going to happen.

My eyes darting back and forth to make sure nobody was nearby, I ran into the store, taking shelter behind large displays of twelve-for-a-dime juice boxes. Then I tippy-toed to the girls' clothing section, where I looked for the most generic clothing I could find.

"How about this?" my mom said, holding up a maroon-and-turquoise-marbled sweater that would be loose on an NFL linebacker.

"No way!" I said. "That won't fit me."

"Find something, then," she would say. "Your dad's coming in ten minutes."

To my parents, ten minutes was ample time to pick your new school wardrobe, since they assumed that to be exactly one new shirt.

Sweat streaming down my face, I scanned my options and cringed as I moved from snowflake-covered sweaters to sweatshirts with teddy bears silk-screened on. When I found a few items I could live with, my dad, finished with his tour of the mall's electronics shop, would come get us, point out a crocheted sweater vest, and exclaim, "I wish my dad could have bought me that when *I* was a kid."

It was a fair point because likely there were kids at our school who were not even getting the discount-store clothes that we were shunning. I'm aware I was an ungrateful brat, but whether it's 1986 or 2011, one constant is that kids are desperate to fit in and I was wholeheartedly one of those kids. Despite the fact that most of our school was all in the same sturdy but rust-covered financial boat, we all still wanted to scamper to the dry shores where you wore Nike shoes or Lacoste shirts. My sisters and I didn't want Sumeet to be ridiculed for his clothes, so we made sure he had Nike shoes. When I had a job in high school, I walked into the two-for-one sale at Beaver Canoe, where the popular kids shopped. I chose one T-shirt in women's medium and the other in boy's XX-small.

Still, although Sumeet had everything I had ever wanted, it didn't seem to be what *he* wanted. In his teenage years, he didn't want flashy clothes with obvious brand names. But because we did, we kept buying them for him. When I told him about my plan to revisit my youth and asked him about his childhood extracurricular activities, he shrugged and said, "A lot of it was pushed on me. Dad pushed soccer on me, you guys signed me up for swimming, and after a while I lost interest."

This stung slightly, mostly that he was bored with opportunities we would have cut off our left braid for. I wondered if perhaps I would have lost interest as well, given the same opportunities. What I looked at as a dream come true he looked at as a chore forced on him by people projecting their own youthful yearnings. Perhaps he was correct, as part of my desire to revisit childhood was definitely a yearning to *finally* have some fun.

Fun wouldn't be the first word that came to mind when describing my childhood. By white standards (Mormons excluded), we were a big family of five offspring. My older sister, two younger sisters, and I all wore our hair in various numbers of braids. This was mostly to help white people tell us apart. My hair was down to my midthigh and braided so tightly in two braids that the part in my hair still remains, after my follicles gave up the fight against my mom's comb. Gurpreet (one braid) and youngest sister Navjit (two braids) had brown eyes, while mine (two braids) were blue and Navroop's (one braid, or two ponytails) were green. Other than that, we likely looked the same to everyone.

The first four years of my life were spent in a two-bedroom apartment with my (two-years-older) sister, Gurpreet, and my parents . . . and my grandmother . . . and my two aunts . . . and my two uncles. It was like a Bombay rooming house in the middle of suburban Canada, but our landlord was kind and turned a blind eye, and that made him happy. My parents took one bedroom, and my sister and I shared the other with our two aunts, who were just teenagers themselves at the time. Each night we snuggled in, one aunt and one niece per double bed, and watched *The Love Boat* on our black-and-white TV set.

Everyone else slept in the living room like a giant third-world slumber party. When my little sister Navroop was born, the decision was made to move to a larger space because we couldn't squeeze another person into our room, and in all honesty, babies are known to cry through all the best parts of cruise-ship comedies.

My mom always told me that I had wished for a younger sister because "I didn't have anyone to play hopscotch with." Gurpreet was an adult, even as a kid, and didn't have any interest in the likes of jumping rope or playing house. She did, however, teach me several songs she learned in kindergarten. This was particularly challenging for me, as I was just learning to speak English from watching television, and after she hit me over the head with a slate for not learning a verse about a witch in a ditch properly, I decided I didn't care for singing all that much.

At that new home, a proper house with a sprawling cherry tree in back, my youngest sister, Navjit, was born. There were now four daughters and no sons—the most undesirable of Indian children ratios. Navjit's birth resulted in days of violent tears on the part of my paternal grandmother, who took equal opportunity loving and hugging her and yelling common Indian grandmother phrases at her like "may you be drowned in cow dung."

The year we moved into that house, I started kindergarten and this is where my academic domination began. I'm not really positive how I did finally learn to speak English, but somehow hours of watching *Three's Company* and *Dallas* taught me the full English language, as well as how to properly manage a family-run oil business while dealing with an alcoholic ex–beauty queen.

It was fairly common for me to achieve straight A's in

grade school. I was rewarded with one dollar for each of these perfect report cards. Although it took me over two years to save for a *Ghostbusters* sticker album, it didn't take long to develop a reputation as a scholastic whiz kid. I was placed in gifted studies in the first grade due to what must have been my superior coloring-within-the-lines skills.

Despite the shoe box of old report cards highlighting my achievements, there was one major blemish on my memories of academic superiority, and because it was published, it was difficult to forget. Everybody has something from their childhood about which they are ashamed—a wetting of the pants, horrifying braces with headgear, the discovery of a secret crush on the principal. My prepubescent Achilles heel comes in the form of a poem; four stanzas that could be deconstructed as closely as *The Inferno* to reveal the confusion in my ten-year-old mind. Each year my school board would compile an anthology, showcasing the best in elementary school poetry. My deft wordsmithing made the cut several years in a row, and here's what appeared in the 1988 edition of the venerable children's poetry book *Within These Covers:*

CHRISTMAS IS COMING
Christmas is coming
So you need more pay.
Let's sit back and remember Jesus
Lying in the hay.
And you can meet Santa Claus
He's so full of life.
Hurry now, he's giving out
Pictures of his wife.

Go to the forest
Dig a tree from the soil.
When you get it home
Decorate it with foil.
It's also time to ask your parents
To work longer shifts.
So they can buy you
Even more expensive gifts.

My pride mostly makes me avoid the exercise, but whenever I do reread the poem, several questions pop into my mind: Where did I get the idea kids wanted pictures of Mrs. Claus? In which issue of *Trailer Living Weekly* did I see a tinfoil-decorated tree?

Why was I giving kids the impression that my parents would agree to work more shifts so I could get a Barbie for Christmas, when I knew that I'd be splitting a box of Turtles chocolates with my sisters, as I did most years?

Mostly, though, I get stuck on the third line. What a glorious and pure message of Christmas: little baby Jesus in the hay. The problem was that I didn't believe in Jesus, and worse still, I didn't know that. Each day at school, I belted out the national anthem of "O Canada," and gave a shout-out to our father who did some sort of art in heaven.

Nowhere during that morning exercise did they explain that this might not be your religion and never did my parents expressly declare to us that we were Sikhs. Sure we went to the Sikh temple (the *gurdwara*) when we were kids, but my parents weren't overly religious, so I thought we were just there because that's where weddings were held and where the best *aloo matar sabji* was prepared.

Besides my fervent devotion to Jesus, the poem reminded me of another thing, made fairly obvious by its message: that I had little idea of self-identity, amid a sea of faces so different from my own.

While the other kids would pull out fruit or potato chips for their recess snack, I would hold mine close to my mouth and eat it as quickly as possible to avoid the inevitable questioning.

"What's that?" a perfect specimen of the Aryan race would ask.

"Oh, it's *barfi,*" I'd say, believing for a minute that they might be interested in trying the sweet Indian delicacy.

"EWWWWW, barf! She's eating barf!"

Even without the taunts, I was aware that what I was eating was unpalatable to my schoolmates. My offers to trade my *jalebi* for their fruit roll-ups were never accepted. So as they shoved chocolate chip cookies into their mouths, I ate fluffy golden sticks of *muttery* during recess. Soon I started bringing cookies myself and ate the *muttery* after school, to be spared the questions.

As my town was mostly German in descent, it celebrated Oktoberfest as if it were a national holiday. As part of the celebration, our school encouraged everyone to dress up in their own ethnic costume.

One festive Oktober in particular stands out in my mind. My mom had pressed and hung both Gurpreet's and my suits the night before so they would be perfect. She had sewn the suits herself, a traditional Punjabi *salwaar/kameez* combination. The *kameezes* were a sunny yellow floral material and accompanied with plain yellow *salwaars* and scarves.

In the morning we got dressed, put our fall jackets and backpacks over our suits, and headed to school. The first thing I noticed upon entering my classroom was that nobody else was dressed up in ethnic garb. I wasn't sure how I hadn't registered that this would be the case, as I was the only ethnic kid in the class. Everyone else was white—and not white but of Scandinavian origin, which meant they could have worn Viking garb, or Scottish enough to have adorned kilts. Most were just third-generation Canadian white, and thus dressed in their native dress of jeans and T-shirts.

I took a deep breath and tried to make it to my desk without being noticed, but as quiet as my steps were, the yellow tropical material shouted out to everyone. As I slid into my desk, jacket still on despite the fact that I was sweating, the oohs and aahs began.

"What a lovely outfit, Rupinder," my teacher said. Now everyone's eyes were fixed on me, which was exactly what I didn't want.

I smiled and was opening my book to my spelling homework when I heard her say, "Why don't you come up here and tell everyone about it?"

My teacher was a very nice woman. She was trying to be kind by showing interest in my culture, but to a seven-year-old, attention for being different is as desirable as a pill that makes you wet yourself during every school assembly. I wished I could pummel through the wall like the Kool-Aid man and make a run for it, but knew that there was no way out of this. I took off my jacket and walked hesitantly to the front of the classroom. Thirty sets of eyes stayed glued upon me as if they were watching a live-action *National Geographic* special.

"Um," I said, realizing I knew nothing of my outfit's significance or history. "It's an Indian suit. Ladies wear it in India."

I rushed back to my seat before questions could be asked.

I prayed that the explanation had satisfied them and that at recess, I would gaze across the school yard and see scores of kids sporting kimonos, saris, and dashikis. Even better would be if one of the school's many German kids had worn an SS uniform, to take some of the heat off me. But when I went into the school yard, everybody but one other poor soul was in his or her normal clothes. Standing against the wall was the matching blindingly yellow suit to mine.

I waved and looked away as some of the girls in my class drew near.

"Cool dress," they said.

"Thanks," I replied, wishing the day were finished so I could run home, change into jeans, and eat salt-and-vinegar chips.

"Can you say something in your language?"

"Um . . . I don't know," I said, hoping the bell was going to ring soon. I had been Indian every other day, too, but something about seeing me in my *salwaar kameez* reminded them that I was different, and that day, I was their new exciting toy.

On a normal day, I would have loved to be the center of their attention, but that day, I didn't feel comfortable with the reason. I felt like a collector's-edition doll they had added to the Barbie collection, a brown-faced friend that "Barbie met on a relief mission with Ken!" and was promoted as coming with "ten different colors of *bindis*!"

"Oh, please, say something!" they all said.

They circled me, begging, and I could have just said ethnic-sounding gibberish or told them that they were horse-faced pigs that smelled of cow manure and they would have been satisfied.

"Say something!" they begged.

I don't know why the bell was always ringing whenever Zack Morris needed to be saved by it on TV, because as I stood there, waiting for them to start tugging at my braids, it was showing me no mercy.

"Say something! Say something!"

This soon turned into a chant until I finally gave in and just sputtered out the Punjabi greeting *Sat-sri-akal*.

"What? Say it again," they said excitedly.

"Say it again! Say something else!"

I wasn't sure what else I could say. I spoke exclusively Punjabi until I was four years old, and then once we plugged a black-and-white television into the wall, a new language was revealed to me and became my preferred mother tongue. Now I spoke Punjabi only when forced. As I was about to spout some random phrases in the hopes of satisfying my classmates, the bell finally chimed and we all rushed in. When I got home, I pulled off my suit and threw it onto the floor.

"Hey," my mom said, seeing the yellow mass of fabric crumpled on my bedroom floor. "Can you hang that up? It took a long time to iron."

I looked at my mom, who was wearing a *salwaar kameez,* as she did every day. She wore them to work, when she left in the morning with her thermos of chai, and she wore them at home, to the mall, and to our parent-teacher conferences. It was the clothing to which she was accustomed and it was the clothing to which I was accustomed to seeing her in. I only wore it when forced, to a wedding, to the *gurdwara,* or to a relative's home, because in my mind, my native dress was the same as the rest of the kids in my class: jeans and a T-shirt.

The next year, my mom asked me, "Are they doing that day again where you wear suits to school?"

"No, they don't do that anymore," I lied.

"That's too bad," she said.

I felt bad lying to her. I wish I had possessed the confidence to wear a suit to school again, to pay tribute to the culture of which my parents were so proud. But I didn't, and for that I felt ashamed. I wanted to at least save my mom the shame of knowing that truth. It was better that she thought it was the school board who was no longer interested in us showcasing our culture than knowing that it was me.

The summer before fifth grade, we moved again, this time just our nuclear family. Aunts and uncles got their own places, as most had succumbed to the time-honored tradition of the arranged marriage. They hopped on planes clutching Canadian passports and returned shortly after with carry-on spouses. The true importance of this segue is that their marriages allowed me to finally get my own room. Personal space is not a virtue in Indian culture, so to have seven cubic feet of my own was like discovering a golden ticket to Willy Wonka's factory. Of course my parents forced me to squeeze a five-piece furniture set into the room, with the dresser pushed up against the bed like a footboard. Still, as I climbed over the side table every night to get into the bed, I didn't have to scream at anybody to turn off the mixed cassette they had taped off the radio so we could sleep.

It was at this new house, in a more middle-class neighborhood than our previous one, that I discovered the categories of "haves" and "have-nots." I undeniably landed in the latter category. My parents liked to tell me that school was not a fashion show, but to a kid, not only is it a fashion show but a beauty pageant, IQ test, fitness assessment, and various other humiliations all rolled into one neat little package marked "Adolescence."

I never had the cool clothes. Not only were my and my siblings' clothes uncool, half of them were homemade or purchased from the fashion capitals of rural India. Our morning outfit choices consisted of dresses made from the same material as our kitchen curtains or separates from such international brands as "Mowgli" and "Star of India." We begged our parents for the same clothes the other kids were wearing, designer camouflage that could help us blend into the crowd. But they refused to budge, so when all of the other kids were wearing perfectly acid-washed jeans and bright polo shirts, we showed up in patchwork pants and leopard-print velour shirts that declared "Kool Kats Klub."

The first year at my new school was also my first introduction to racism, although I didn't know it at the time. Some classmates and I were standing in a circle telling jokes, most of which had been overheard from adults or older kids. A girl named Lisa was up next and assured us that she had a doozy of a joke but first needed to know a bit of information.

"Is anyone here a Paki?"

I had no idea what that word meant or whom it referenced. Neither did Lisa. We all looked at one another, shook our heads no, and she continued on. The gist of the joke was that you would take a bowl of water and pour in salt, which signified white people. Then you would add pepper to signify black people, and the two would mingle at the surface of the water. Then you would add some cinnamon. This represented the "Pakis" in question. Upon the entry of the cinnamon into the water, the other two spices would float quickly away from it. We all giggled slightly, though the joke was weak with the absence of visual aids. But, Lisa assured us, wherever she had seen it enacted, it garnered some big laughs. It wasn't until two years later that I realized whom the term *Paki* referenced, when someone shouted it at my sisters and me as we played in a park.

We had gone to visit our cousin who lived in a suburb of Toronto. The suburb was a lot more multicultural than our town, which helped build cultural identities but also created racial tensions as big groups of different ethnicities struggled for footholds.

As we all played soccer in a nearby park, we heard someone shouting from the street that lined it. Two teenagers were on their dirt bikes and looking in our direction. We couldn't hear what they were saying but we knew it was directed at us.

"What did they say?" I asked Gurpreet.

"I don't know," she said.

As Navroop, Navjit, and our little cousin came running toward us, we all heard it loud and clear.

"Pakis!" the boys shouted. "Dirty Pakis!"

We were all shocked and stood there frozen as they laughed. If they chose to ride their bikes down the hill toward us, there would be nothing we could do and nobody who could help us. Luckily the boys kept biking right past us, and once they were out of sight, we all ran back to my cousin's house and never told our parents what happened.

At the same time that Sumeet was losing interest in childhood lessons, my sisters and I were continuing our only available leisure activity—watching TV. Most of our viewing was done in the basement, where we could watch in peace. Two sofas sat a foot from the back walls and created a *V*, with such intricate floral patterns on them that your allergies could act up at the mere sight. The wood paneling on the walls had only been inflicted on half of the basement, the other half's walls maintaining their original drywall charm.

Behind one sofa, on the unfinished ceiling that let us hear every movement in the kitchen above, a coatrack hung, filled with coats that had no purpose but to make our house look like a swap meet. Below them was a veritable repository of used housewares—old toys, a dismantled crib, and piles of blankets. Whenever I visit home now, I have to shield my eyes from the visual assault when I enter the basement. But back then, our eyes were glued only to the television screen, twenty-seven inches of escapism in a box, set atop another television, which, despite no longer working and being wood veneered, was still not deemed trash.

This is what we did while other kids were out on the weekends having fun. While our classmates spent Friday nights at house parties, we were on the bridge of the starship *Enterprise* yelling, "Look out behind you, Worf!" to the screen. As our classmates went out on dates, we watched *The Golden Girls*.

"Home again on a Saturday night?" Blanche would tease Dorothy. Yes, we would all nod along. Like Dorothy, we spent every night of the weekend at home. Indian parents have a somewhat ironic fear of sexuality, considering that their culture offered the world the Kama Sutra. Not only was there no dating in my household, there was no talk of dating. Luckily, this was no problem, since we pretty much lived in our basement and it was fairly difficult to meet guys there. So we watched TV.

When we weren't watching TV, we had to clean.

The whole place was covered in a protective layer. The sofas had dustcovers on them. The table had a vinyl tablecloth . . . topped with a clear plastic tablecloth . . . atop which sat place mats. Every lampshade in our house was still encased in its plastic cover. Our house looked like a furniture shrine. I spent half of my childhood expecting my parents to put red velvet barricades around the furniture and hire a docent to whisper, "Please step back from the coffee table."

An outing now and then was permitted, as long as my parents didn't have to drive, but even this warranted a barrage of questions.

"Who are you going with? What are you going to see? Isn't there an earlier movie?"

After a while we just saved ourselves the exhaustion and stopped asking. Even if we made it to a party, we would have to keep checking our watches and have someone drive us home at nine, before most of the other kids had even arrived. This was so much more conspicuous than not being there at all.

Ironically, although we always had to decline, the requests still poured in. We were thankful just to be socially nominated, but this required speeches more rehearsed than those at the Oscars.

When I was out to lunch with Navjit recently, she reminded me of an integral social survival tactic of our teenage years. "I just knew to not ask for anything," she said, wolfing down her veggie burger. "I knew to say no to any invite I got and I learned how to make lame excuses about why I couldn't do things."

I always thought that Navjit had it the roughest. She was six years younger than me, and seeing three older siblings already go through the motions of wanting things they would not get, she didn't even bother. She made herself content with having little. She wore three sets of hand-me-downs, and while other kids spent summers at camp, she was pleased to be at home and do the book reports I would assign to keep her sharp over the summer. She would read an old book we had lying around, and synopsize it for me in a report. When we ran out of books, I assigned her a stack of old *Reader's Digests*.

Until she said it at lunch, I had almost forgotten the lies

that were the cornerstone of our teenage years. If I had a dime for every time I said our aunt was over, our relatives were visiting from out of town, and a cousin had a birthday, I would have the net worth of Warren Buffett.

I was so casual about dropping my various prior-engagement excuses that I would never have thought that my friends still remembered them fifteen years later.

"How many cousins' birthday parties could you have had?" my friend Jill said.

"One year we thought we should track all of the cousins' birthdays to see if they lined up year to year," Stacey added.

Oddly enough, their perception of this excuse was not that I wasn't allowed to go out, but that I wasn't really interested in going out with them. Nothing could have been further from the truth. Not only were my friends fun, smart, and kind, they were the most popular girls in our grade. I often wondered if I had made a pact with the devil in my sleep to gain a spot in their group, but I figured I could sort that out in the afterlife. I was never able to see them out of school hours, so I wasn't sure why they still kept me around and now here they were, wondering what it was I didn't like about them.

"You never blamed not going out on your parents," Stacey said. "So I figured you just weren't into whatever we were doing."

"I guess sometimes I wondered if you didn't really like us as much as you seemed to," my friend Melodie said. "Because you would usually just say that 'you can't' and not something like 'my parents are being totally unfair and won't let me.'"

While I was growing up, honesty was not the best policy

for me. I never let on that my parents were strict, because it was so humiliating. I thought that there was no way my friends could understand my parents and their overprotection. I just assumed my friends knew and that we were all avoiding talking about it because it was embarrassing to me. I would never have believed that the real reason they didn't bring it up was that they were hurt. I wish I could have been more honest as a teenager, but I just wanted to sweep my strict upbringing under the rug.

It was always perplexing just what exactly my parents thought would happen if they let us loose once in a while. Despite all of my parents' worries and concerns for the influences that would persuade us to follow them down dark paths, they had no reason to have ever worried. My grades were phenomenal, but I think they could have actually been better if I had been given the benefit of a balanced social life. I often left my homework until the last minute because my whole life felt like one big chore. I had to dry the dishes and babysit my brother on Friday nights. I already felt as if I was living a life devoid of fun, so the last thing I wanted to do was sit down to an hour's worth of math homework. If I knew I could go to a party or watch movies at Stacey's after a week of working nonstop at home and at school, I would have worked relentlessly toward that goal. But I had no such carrot dangled in front of me, just the faint scent of *gajar daal* emanating from under my fingernails.

I was never going to recover whatever fun I had missed socializing like a normal teenager. In fact, I knew I was never going to be able to go back in time and give myself a childhood out of an Indian *Full House* spin-off, but it would be fun to shake up my routine and learn something new while ticking off a wish list that was decades old. I was taking the better-late-than-never approach to adolescence, and though the fine lines around my eyes indicated that I was definitely north of "late," there was no time like the present.

→ TWO ←

the little indian mermaid

Now that I had committed to my plan and had a list of things to do over the year, I was itching to get right down to it.

"Don't worry," my friend Jaclyn told me as we sat in a food court one bitter winter day. "I'll teach you how to swim. I was a lifeguard for four summers."

Jaclyn, Jen (who now also happened to be my downstairs neighbor), and I were all publicists at a television company. For some very odd reason, people often asked Jaclyn and me if we were sisters. We both had dark hair and blue eyes, so I guess people thought the fact that we were two different races was merely a detail. Had Naomi Campbell been standing with us and wearing blue contacts, I'm sure they would have thrown her into the mix. Our love of fluorescent lighting often led the three of us to the food court for a break from talking and breathing TV.

"That's not the issue," I said, dumping half my stir-fry into Jen's plate. "So many people have offered to teach me. I just need time." Swimming was, beyond a shadow of a doubt, the scariest proposition on my list.

At our old house, there was a neighborhood pool nearby. It was a small outdoor pool that reached a maximum depth of four feet, but to my sisters and me it was like plummeting into the ocean depths. A few times each summer, when our parents gave in to our tireless begging, we would each scour the house for the dime you needed for entry and go there to spend the day with all of the other neighborhood kids. It was perfect because the pool was so packed that nobody was actually swimming. This meant that our standing in the water gripping the edge of the shallow end didn't attract any attention.

In the fifth grade, my class took swimming lessons for six weeks. Most of the kids could already swim, so I was left in a motley group of beginners. During the first class it looked as if not one of us would swim a stroke in our lives, but by the second class, everybody but me was slowly floating along. At ten, my issue was not fear but a simple lack of the necessary mechanics. My body didn't know to stay straight to float. It refused to simultaneously retain oxygen and maintain calm.

The instructor didn't know what to do with me.

"Why don't you practice here?" she said finally, giving me two jugs of water that were meant to act as de facto flotation devices. The rest of the group moved on to the deeper waters while I tried to leverage my weight onto the water jugs and become one with the pool. It was proving difficult. More difficult than that was swimming with two rope swings hanging from my head.

After our swimming class, the other girls would change and quickly put their heads under the dryer before we could head out into the Canadian winter.

I, on the other hand, would need the full school day for the heat to penetrate the mass of my hair. After the second class, I realized that I could not dry the hair right in the braid, and to the cheers of my classmates, I unraveled my Rapunzel plaits to dry my knee-length locks. I knew I might get in trouble with my mom, who would have to redo them, but the kids were fawning over me like they had just found out I was a foreign princess. I would just tell my mom that my elastics fell out, because a few hours of popularity was worth the risk.

On the fourth lesson, I still could not swim an inch but was gaining popularity because of the excitement that would come with me letting down my hair. "Take it out now," one tiny blond girl suggested before the lesson. "You're just going to take them out later."

I was like their little Indian mermaid and couldn't disappoint my fans, so she and I took an elastic each and unfurled both of my braids.

"Wow," the whole class said as I walked out onto the deck.

This was a brilliant strategy for me. To deflect attention from the fact that I could not swim, I would distract everyone with my pretty hair. This worked well for one more lesson until a group of senior citizens swarmed me after their aquacize class.

"Oh my," one of the ladies said, eyeing my tresses. "Do they let you into the pool like that?"

"Um, yeah," I muttered, unsure of what the correct answer was.

"It's not very safe," one of her cohorts chimed in. "You could get caught in the drain."

This drain was not anything I had ever considered when making the decision to undo my braids. Peer pressure was a more powerful motivator than personal safety, but the idea of getting caught in the pool drain and missing our year-end trip to the local water park scared the vanity out of me. After this, I kept my hair tightly wound in its braids and stayed clear of the edges when walking around with my water jugs. Luckily I had a lot of space to maneuver, since the rest of my group was in the deep end with the others. I made it to the water park, where I spent the day standing in the shallow end. That was one of my last times in a public pool.

Twenty years later, I was finally ready to give it another try. Oprah learned to swim at forty, so I would actually be a decade ahead of her in that achievement. Not to make myself a hero but I'd be learning in a public pool, where my body and numerous screams for help would be exposed to the unsuspecting masses. Oprah, meanwhile, likely learned it in the privacy of her giant pool while Maya Angelou read her inspirational quotes and Stedman fixed them all iced tea. But we both had the goal of learning to swim, and by Gayle I was going to achieve it.

But first, there was some preparation required. Ten-year-olds don't have to spend their time planning for swimming by looking up "knee-length swimsuits" for days before. It wasn't vanity as much as it was a safety issue. The ripple created by my legs hitting the water could startle my fellow novice swimmers. My thighs could be mistaken for floatation devices and cause confusion in rescue simulations. But mostly, I couldn't stomach being stared at by six-year-olds in water wings when flutter boards got caught in the folds of my flesh. And so what?

No woman this side of the cast of *Baywatch* feels good in a bathing suit. So before the swimming could begin, some slimming had to begin.

I was putting it off anyway. You would never think I was fat to look at me, but if you passed my desk at work and saw my thumb pulling the elastic of my tights off my stomach as I read *Variety,* you might think twice. Also, shocking even to me, at my last yearly physical, my doctor took my height and weight, did a quick calculation, and kindly let me know that I was indeed a porker.

"What?!" I said, worried my big butt jokes had created a self-fulfilling prophecy. I always felt I had a few pounds to lose, but I was nowhere close to doing interviews on *Donahue* via satellite from my bed. "I must have been slouching during the height check. Let me stand straighter."

My doctor gave me a pitying look but agreed to try it again. The two subsequent measurements also revealed the prognosis of plumpness. "Try to lose five or ten pounds," she said. "That's all you need to lose."

A lifetime of chip bowls had finally caught up with me. I

don't know why I thought I could outrun the effects of junk food as I got winded walking from the kitchen to the sofa. Okay, I thought, why not up the ante on this self-improvement journey? If I was going to relive the past, I might as well improve the present while I was at it.

Going to the gym regularly makes you feel like a million dollars. Returning to the gym after months of absence makes you feel like a sumo wrestler in a biathlon. Walking to the gym that first time back, I was proud of myself for making the pledge for a better me, but once I got there, I grew worried that someone I knew, a mortal enemy from my past, would see me in my "before" stage. Adding to my anxiety was the fact that I chose to return to fitness at unequivocally the worst time of the year—January. I stared over at the cardio room, bursting at the seams with sweaty masses in their new Christmas workout clothes, and shook my head, scoffing at the New Year's resolution crowd. The fact that I was one of them was beside the point.*

Hopping onto the stair climber, I looked over my shoulder and covered the keypad while punching in my weight, the way banks advise you to do when using the ATM. I set the timer for forty minutes, pressed play on my *GET SKINNY!* playlist, and climbed like I was James Bond trying to beat an Eastern European villain to the top of the CN Tower. After what seemed like an eternity, my legs near collapse and my heart three pumps short of a coronary, I looked down at the timer. Six minutes. This was going to be a long road to the pool.

*Any facts that make me seem common, stupid, or hypocritical will hereby be considered to be beside the point.

→ THREE ←

perfect strangers (me and rhythm)

At our junior high talent shows, all of the beautiful dancers would dazzle the crowd by doing splits in the air and prancing around in their glittery bodysuits. I just sat watching enviously and waiting for the inevitable Salt-N-Pepa airband, where kids would advise us to "push it." I begged to take dance lessons several times, but was never allowed. Indian girls don't wear leotards and entertain crowds.

Navroop and Navjit refused to muzzle their rhythm and decided to open their own dance studio in the basement. The studio had exactly two students, who also happened to be the two instructors.

They practiced routines in the basement for hours and hours. Whenever Gurpreet and I tried to go downstairs, their fingers would hit the PAUSE button on their boom box.

"We have to practice!" Navjit would say. "We have a show next week!"

The show in question was for Gurpreet and me, and the next week we sat on one of the sofas in the basement, ready for the big debut. The other sofa had been pulled in front of the TV to create a stage of sorts. The dancers, wearing their normal sweatsuits that they had jazzed up with beaded necklaces, came out from behind the sofa and took center stage.

"Thank you for coming," Navjit said. "We hope you enjoy the show." She signaled over to Navroop, who hit PLAY on their music and the sweet sounds of New Kids on the Block filled the room. They were thirty seconds into "The Right Stuff" when Navjit turned the wrong way on a spin.

"Other way!" Navroop said.

They recovered, but at the beginning of the Jordan Knight solo dance, Navroop took a false step and knocked into Navjit.

"Watch it!" Navjit said.

The performers took a brief break behind their sofa curtain and soon began arguing.

"You're Danny!" Navroop said.

"No, you're Danny!" Navjit replied.

The show had to end its run that night when the principal dancers started choking each other behind their curtain. I doubted this ever happened in the Alvin Ailey dance company.

Still, my desire to dance survived the Basement Dance Company debacle. After some recommendations from my work friends, I sent a quick note to a downtown studio asking when their winter schedule would be released. Five minutes later, my in-box dinged with a response sent from Esther.

"Hi, Rupinder! Thank you for your interest! Our new class schedule is now posted! Let me know if you need anything!" Wow, I thought, that is quite a lot of exclamation points. Perhaps her other options for punctuation were all gummed on the keyboard, leaving her only with the option of exclaiming everything, in a tone that could only be created in a face-to-face conversation by punching someone in the mouth after each sentence. When I responded to say I was interested, Esther proclaimed, "Awesome! I put you on the list! Have a great day!"

Finally, I was going to be a dancer. I imagined myself smiling all the time, kicking my heels up high when I walked, and calling everything "fantabulous." My fellow dancers and I would compete against one another for chorus-line roles while dealing with the pressures of being young and taut gazelles. I would collapse on the floor in a cascade of tears after a fight with my boyfriend/dance partner. And in my greatest triumph, through the pain of a swollen ankle, I would dance flawlessly in the finals of the dance competition while my friends pumped their fists in the air for support. Pushing his way through a cheering crowd, a Billy Hufsey type would hoist me on his shoulders while Debbie Allen glided through the air in a celebratory split. I wrote Esther back, "Thanks! I can't wait!"

On the day of my first tap class, a woman met me in the parking lot beside my office. I handed her ten dollars and she handed me a package. A man getting out of his minivan eyed me suspiciously, so I opened the package to show that the goods inside were a lightly worn pair of old tap shoes. I took them upstairs, put them on, and performed an impromptu dance for my coworkers in our kitchen. Only one shoe had a shoelace but I still put on a decent performance while humming "Tea for Two" to myself.

"Good luck!" everyone yelled as I ran out of the office that night. Our department was 90 percent women, which provided a Ya-Ya Sisterhood of sorts.

"Thanks," I said, throwing a pile of DVDs onto my colleague's desk. "Watch those," I yelled to her as I ran for the elevator. "We can talk about story angles in our meeting tomorrow." But tonight, the story was me.

Arriving at my first class, I started to feel the reality of my grand experiment and it was exciting. I was going to learn to dance. The first thing I noticed was that everyone had black standard tap shoes with laces, whereas mine were cream Mary Janes with pink ribbon laces. Note to self: Spend more than ten dollars on equipment next time.

The style made my love of loud festive socks difficult to hide. I tried to put one foot atop the other, but that only made the pink socks with penguins on them more visible. I saw a girl beside me looking at them curiously and I laughed nervously and pretended to be doing some stretches, one of which almost punctured the eye of the girl to my right.

Perhaps because I am not very worldly, I was surprised that there were two men in the class, and not two men in spandex. They both looked to be in their midtwenties and as if they had just finished their shifts as IT specialists and just wanted to tap before going home and devouring a porterhouse.

"Hi," I said to one of the guys, "I'm Rupinder."

"Hi," he said. "Is this your first time in the class?"

"Yes," I said, worried. "Isn't it just starting tonight?"

"Oh yes," he said. "I just took some of the classes in the fall, then had to stop after the accident."

He paused dramatically after saying "the accident" like Victor Newman would have done in *The Young and the Restless*.

"Oh, okay," I said, deciding to deny my curiosity the chance to ask more. "I hope it's fun."

Two girls walked in and stood directly in front of me. One was tiny and looked as if her outfit choice had taken her the full day preceding the class. The spandex pants were cuffed in the same color of green as her tight tank top and she had clipped her hair off her face, revealing a pair of dangling earrings. I felt suddenly self-conscious about my loose sweatpants and bulky sweatshirt embroidered with the logo for the Food Network.

"Hi," I said to them while they laced up their shoes. The small one looked up. The other one looked away. I took it personally for exactly three seconds before I saw that the instructor had just walked in, tall, dark, and handsome. He looked like Taye Diggs, and the faces of my classmates revealed that many of the ladies were looking to get their groove back.

"Hi, everyone, I'm Jerry," he said, tapping out a simple rhythm. "Everyone ready to tap into their inner Fred Astaire?" Jerry looked as if he was five years younger than I was and danced so gracefully that you could imagine him dancing his way out of the birth canal while "Fly Me to the Moon" played in the delivery room. "This is a basic tap," he instructed, striking his foot on the floor. I followed along and loved the sound. *Tap. Tap. Tappity Tap. Tap. Tap.* It was intoxicatingly melodic.

Oh, the joy of learning something new—exhilaration and humiliation all rolled into one. As the class progressed, I stared intently at myself in the mirror as I shuffled to the right and tapped to the left. With each click and clack of my shoes, I was beginning to feel like a real certified dancer instead of just a woman in sweatpants dancing in a basement.

→ FOUR ←

no animal house

Navroop, who was determined to be a dog owner or at least a dog aunt, was solely focused on helping me cross the goal of pet ownership off my list.

"Okay," she began when I picked up the phone one night. "I e-mailed three breeders for you. One has a litter of Westies due in two months and one has Japanese Chins that were born three weeks ago. One boy is left."

"Oh, thanks," I said. "But I don't know if I can do this that fast. I really want to think about it."

"Don't worry," she said. "The last one has a litter of some sort of doodle that they're expecting in four months. Then you have more time."

"Even that seems fast to me," I explained. "I was thinking more like six or eight months."

"Oh, fine." Navroop relented. "But then I don't think I can help anymore. I get too attached. Just call me when you have a dog."

I knew Navroop thought I was indecisive, but this was not a skirt I could return the next day. This was a living, breathing, drooling decision that was going to live with me for the next fifteen years. We had to be right for each other. Would a small dog fit best in my life? It would be happiest in apartment living, not need as much food, and fit in my bike basket as I jaunted through the South of France, holding baguettes and waving at men named Jacques. But a big dog has always been more my style. With small dogs, there is always the chance that I will turn into one of those crazy women who buys her Yorkie drop earrings or ends up on a talk-show intervention after being seen sharing a milk shake with two straws with her Chihuahua.

A big dog always felt right to me. Old Spot or Rover or Mr. Furr-ley would lie at my feet calmly while I lounged on the sofa watching a *Perfect Strangers* marathon. I would put one of those barrels around its neck like in cough-syrup commercials and train it to go into the kitchen, grab me a Pepsi, and shove a pawful of Doritos into the barrel. With a decision this big, I decided that small steps were the best route, especially considering the Gill history of pet ownership.

When I was growing up, every two months or so over a five-year stretch, an opportunity would arise to bring up the subject of getting a dog. No matter how small the window, my sisters and I could get on all fours and attempt to squeeze through it.

The attempts went from timid:

A dog appears on a television commercial. Mom either grimaces or smiles.

Kid: "Wow, that is a cute dog. I would love to have one too." Gap-toothed smile.

To ridiculous:

Mom: "Someone dry the dishes!"

Kid: "You know, I just watched a news program that showed how they taught dogs in Japan to do housework. It really helped with household chores."

To desperate:

Mom: "Go check on your brother."

Kid: "He is gone! We had better go get a search-and-rescue dog so we can always know where he is. It is imperative for his safety!"

It never worked. When I was twelve years old, my pocket burning with ten dollars saved from ten weeks of allowance, I decided to take matters into my own hands. My parents would not allow a dog, but after some convincing, they agreed to a fish. My dad drove me down to the neighborhood Walmart, where I sprinted to the pet department, pressed my face against the aquariums, and after much deliberation chose two goldfish. I took them home, christened them Moby Dick and Cleo, put my elbows up on my dresser, and stared at them for hours.

"Let me see!" Navjit squealed in her shrill four-year-old's voice.

"Don't touch them!" I screamed, pulling Navjit's fingers out of the bowl. "You can't pet fish."

"Then what do they do?" she asked earnestly.

"They swim, dummy," know-it-all Navroop said.

My dad walked by on his way to his own room and saw the commotion.

"Don't forget to feed them," he said in the tone he later used for such "don't" expressions as "Don't forget to lock the door" after I had lived in the city for nearly five years, and his oft-repeated "Don't trust the banks, they are all crooks."

"Yes, I know," I said as Navjit continued to try to brush her fingers against the fish's fins. "I wrote it all down. Now everyone get out of here. I have work to do."

The work I had to do was staring at the fish. In those subsequent hours, I realized something critical: fish do very little. And by very little I mean nothing. But that gave us a kinship of sorts. I lived in a slightly bigger bowl but had about the same level of excitement in my day that they did.

Nonetheless, as boring as their lives were, those fish were mine, all mine. It turned out that I wasn't the only one in my family who was enamored with them. Although my dad refused to ever let me have a pet that could survive outside a bowl, he came into my room every hour that night to see that the fish were okay. He also thought that the incredibly complicated daily needs of a fish (feed once) were too taxing for a ten-year-old, so despite my assurances that I had it covered, he kindly fed them their fish food without telling me. Straight out of a *Three's Company* story line, I fed them again myself later that same day.

The next morning I woke up to find them both floating in the bowl, one with a bloody nose and the other just seemingly unwilling to live a life of being constantly stared at and overfed.

"Oh," my dad said, looking at their bodies floating around the bowl. "I wonder what happened. I fed them."

"So did I!" I screamed. "I told you I was going to feed them."

"I thought you would forget," he said.

Eight weeks of allowance on two fish, a bowl, the upgraded pretty blue gravel, and extra-protein fish food. Wasted. I was upset but aware that the stress of our household was probably too much for any living thing. I don't recall who disposed of the fish but there was no ceremony, like sitcom kids always hold. I cleaned out the bowl and shoved it on a shelf in the garage, where it still remains more than twenty years later.

Later my dad told me a story that illustrated that fish ownership was not in the genes.

"When I was eight or nine," he began, "I went down to the village creek.

"If you stirred the mud up," he explained, whirring his arms to show the motion, "the fish would all come to the top of the water.

"I took off all of my clothes and jumped in and stirred the water," he said.

"When the fish came up, I grabbed one and put it in my pocket. It was a hot, sunny day and I walked home so excited, almost forty minutes. Bibi had bought me a nice new metal dish, and when I got home, I put the fish in the dish with some water. When I woke up the next day, everybody asked what the smell was. It was so bad that we had to throw out both the fish and the kettle."

It was obvious that a fish would never survive more than a day in any Gill household, but when I was in college, my sisters, brother, and I sat down and decided to go big. It was time to stop working ourselves up the pet ladder. We were going to go right to the top of it and finally get a dog. There was some concern because when the dog would be three or four, none of us girls would live at home anymore, leaving Sumeet with the responsibility. But we finally had the money to do it and thought it would be a nice companion for my brother, so we decided to go ahead with it and would deal with the parents later.

"What do you think they will say?" Navroop asked.

"Who cares?" Gurpreet said. "They can live with it. If we just do it, they will have to deal with it."

We pondered this as we ripped open a giant bag of salt-and-vinegar chips. Chips always made us think more clearly.

"I don't know," I said. "This is a big risk to take in case they don't accept it. Then what do we do?"

We decided to err on the side of foolish optimism. Our parents were old and had so many kids, so our hope was that they wouldn't even notice an addition. Or perhaps they would grow fond of their new canine housemate. All they ever wanted was an obedient child, and no matter how good we were, we would never fetch their slippers.

After Navroop found us a reputable breeder of chocolate Labs, I sent an e-mail.

"Hello, Claire," I wrote. "We are a lovely family of seven who live in a beautiful quiet suburb and would like to add a member of your family to ours. (Preferably a dog.) Yours most sincerely, Miss Rupinder Gill."

The attempt at humor must have sealed the deal, as she wrote back and notified me that we could reserve a puppy in their upcoming litter. I sent off a check for a hundred dollars, and with that, we were e-mailed a picture of her last group of puppies, frolicking in a field. We looked at the photo over and over again for weeks.

"What are we naming it?" Navjit asked, aware of the firestorm this question would bring.

"I had better get out the registry," Navroop said.

The registry was a list of names that Navroop maintained. If you came up with a name that you wanted to save for a future pet, child, car, etc., you had to alert Navroop so she could add it to the registry under your name. The name was henceforth yours until such time as you relinquished it or bartered it for another. It was our rudimentary system of copyrighting.

Many votes and brainstorm sessions resulted in a winning name: Jefferson.

Jefferson was the name of a hamster Sumeet brought home for the Christmas break of his first grade in school. After a day, he lost interest in it, and my mother, worried about being branded as the family that killed Jefferson, took over his care. She could be seen around the house, scrounging for toilet-paper rolls for Jefferson's midmorning recess.

After months of anticipation, the big day finally came. An e-mail arrived in my in-box announcing that the new puppies had been born. The Gill house was in a flurry. But it was a very muffled flurry, because we were hiding it from the actual owners of the house.

My siblings made an appointment to visit the breeders and choose our new member of the family. I was away at college so couldn't go and called for the report.

"Well?" I asked excitedly on the phone as they were driving home.

"They were sooo cute!" Navjit yelled into the phone. "They all just kept running up to me."

"There was one that liked me the best," Navroop said. "I think that one's Jefferson. Yes, that's definitely Jefferson."

They kept speaking over each other to tell me their fond recollections of the newest family member.

A few hours later we all spoke again for a final check of details, and the reality of taking care of a dog finally hit us. Inevitably, our parents WOULD soon notice something barking in the living room. My mom noticed every time that we hid one of her fifteen silk flower arrangements in the living room, so this was unlikely to escape her notice. We had to let the dream go.

Navroop was the most crushed, as she wanted a dog more than any of us. In anticipation, she had already bought a leash, having counted her puppies before they hatched.

"We'll never get a dog," Navroop said when I came home for the weekend.

"You can get one when you get your own place," I said, looking for the silver lining.

"Oh, who cares then?" she said. "I want one now. You want one when you're a kid."

She took the leash she had bought and put it away in a box under her bed. It was like her trousseau for her future dog, which she'd been planning for since the age of five.

Not having met little Jefferson myself, I was the least affected and sent a note off to the breeder full of tiny white lies.

"Hi, Claire," I wrote. "Unfortunately we can no longer get one of your lovely puppies, as our grandparents are moving in with us."

Claire was gracious and e-mailed to say how wonderful it was that we would have that opportunity. She must have known it was a lie, as nobody sits down to decide between getting a Lab or having Grandma move in instead, but in any case, we were off the hook with the minor casualties of a lost deposit and five broken hearts.

It had been ten years since the Jefferson fiasco so this time I was determined to do my homework. Before getting up the hopes of my sisters and myself yet again, I needed to do some preliminary legwork. Like a new bride already reading parenting books, I made an appointment with an allergist. My eyes welded shut if I was in the same room as a cat, so I wanted to make sure this didn't extend to dogs. Why agonize over a decision that might not even be a possibility for me? Arriving at the office, I opened the door to discover what had become of Morticia Addams, who had spent the seventies as a roadie for Kiss, then become a receptionist for Dr. Albert Heywood, allergist.

With stark black hair and bloodred lips drawn upon the palest of lily-white skin, she looked up at me through her feathered bangs and said, "How can I help you?" Her voice alluded to how I could help her—by slipping her a nicotine patch.

"Um, I have an allergy test scheduled," I stammered, waiting for Cousin Itt to come out of a back room. I felt as if my allergies to something were already acting up. Perhaps that was part of the test, or perhaps they needed to invest in a feather duster or sandblaster to remove the foot of dust that lined the tops of all of the furniture.

"Go right in," she rasped, and ushered me into the doctor's office.

I'm not good at guessing people's ages, but I would estimate that Dr. Heywood was between 200 and 250 years old. His office looked as if it had last been cleaned after the First World War, then bombed in the Second World War. Shuffling behind his desk, he motioned to two stained chairs and invited me to sit down. Quickly calculating which of the two would have less likelihood of a bedbug infestation, I sat down gingerly on the edge of one of them.

Looking at my chart, he said, "Rupinder, is that Sikh?" When I nodded, he said, "Where's your little hat?" and patted his head like monkeys did in old black-and-white films. Did he just ask me where my hat was? I was so surprised I almost fell off my chair; also because a bitchy cockroach was trying to push me off it.

"Do you mean a turban?" I said. "That's for men. And only really religious men." What a notion—that I would wake up each morning, wash my gargantuan head of hair, blow-dry it, straighten it, and then . . . shove it under a turban. Did he think I had a denim turban for casual Friday, a light stretch wool turban for work meetings, and Burberry-tartan turban for after-work drinks? I held my tongue. I was here for a purpose. Think of the puppies, think of the puppies.

Quickly changing the subject, he asked me the reason for my visit and I explained my desire to get a dog. I thought that he would praise me for my forethought, but he decided to take a different route. "WHY?" he said with a look of disgust. "Then you have no freedom. And you don't even have a husband to help you." It was a quick segue from my religion to my lack of a mate. I didn't know if he was joking or not, but I didn't care to get caught in this particular conversation. Being hassled about being thirty and unmarried was a conversation I saved to enjoy with all my middle-aged relatives. I wasn't going to enter into it with a nonrelative who was less middle-aged and more from the Middle Ages.

Seeing my frown, he suggested we get to the actual test. After cutting little lines on my back with a tiny blade and creating a Morse-code pattern on it, Dr. Heywood proceeded to inject each hole full of a variety of irritants to see if anything could irritate me more than his commentary. The itch was indescribable, as dust and pollen and cat dander oozed into my body. I clenched the table tightly to avoid jumping up and rubbing my back furiously against a desk corner. As I expected, my back flared up with the presence of cats . . . and pollen . . . but sigh, thank heavens, it was calm in the presence of dogs. Not allergic.

"Okay, thanks," I said, the itch now consuming me. I pulled down my T-shirt and jumped off the table. As I was putting on my jacket, the itch intensified, now trapped under layers of clothing, no air to soothe it.

"Don't scratch," Dr. Heywood cautioned. "You will want to, but don't."

"Of course," I said, fully intending to take off all of my clothes on the subway and scratch my back with a pen in my bag. "Bye."

On the way out, Morticia said, "Have a nice day" more as a challenge than a good-bye. I couldn't help eyeballing her nails, those beautiful long scratching tools. I wanted to grab them and run them over my back, but maintained my composure. As I ran out of the office, I thought of puppies, with long scratchy nails on their paws.

The perfect opportunity for a canine test run arose a couple of months later. I was taking a staycation, which was great. But I wasn't going away because I had no money to go anywhere, which was less great. This provided an opportunity to finally hang the pictures that had been collecting dust for a year in my closet and take care of important tasks like alphabetizing my breakfast cereals. With me at home, and Jaclyn's new puppy, Tucker, home alone just blocks away, it was also the perfect time to test out a dog in the house. I picked him up at 8 A.M. and ran him home in my arms because his Yorkie paws were too small to jump the freshly filling puddles. At 10 A.M. he woke up from his nap on my bed. From ten to eleven he sat on my lap as I worked on my computer, and at 11 A.M. he parked himself in front of the television to catch up with the cast of *The View*.

It seemed too easy. Tucker was everything I always wanted in a dog—a cute and calm little love bug. This made me think for one moment that I too could have a calm dog. Then my mind went to its comfort zone of the worst-case scenario and painted my canine future, a picture uglier than the one you see of the dogs playing poker.

In this blurry dream sequence, I would happen upon a basket of Weimaraners and choose the happiest-looking pup of the lot. I would take him home, christen him Dwayne

Wayne, and set him down to survey his new home. He would look up at me happily, wag his little tail, then tear into the living room and proceed to destroy it like the Tasmanian Devil. He would jump on the sofa, pee all over it, then rip up the cushions. His tiny puppy teeth would uproot my plants, pull the stuffing from my chairs, and chew up my phone.

Spotting my important papers, he would run over, change vital information, and walking over to my laptop, disable the firewall and e-mail photos of me from my Frosh 15 phase to various handsome old acquaintances. He would deprogram my PVR, erasing all of the *Frasier*s I have been saving for my Friday-night treat, and pull apart my bookshelves, tearing the pages from the spines and judging me for the Sidney Sheldons I had hidden behind the Tolstoys.

I would try to obedience train him and he would yell, "You're not my mother!" and slam the doggy door. After being awoken by him every morning at 5 A.M. because he wanted to go out for a walk and tell me about his "strange dream involving Ted Danson and a Christmas ham," I would wander bleary-eyed into the washroom to get ready for work. All the while he would look at my outfit and make comments like "It's nice that you don't worry about appearances anymore."

I snapped out of it when Tucker climbed up onto my lap. On the one hand, there were so many stories of people returning or abandoning dogs because they became too much work. On the other, dogs were so sweet, and so eager to please. Surely it would be okay? My wavering about getting a dog was starting to annoy everyone, most of all me. I wanted Snoopy, but was terrified I would get Cujo.

→ FIVE ←

trying-to-stop-growing pains

Three weeks into tapping, I was feeling the strain on my legs. I feared this would be an issue. One of the reasons kids can dance, do track, skip rope, swim, and basically keep their bodies in a constant calorie-burning state is that they don't have early osteoarthritis and vein-covered knees.

Also, a lifetime of junk-food addiction had made me a bit sluggish. When I was growing up, the four food groups on our nutritional chart were: chocolate, fast food, chips, and soft drinks. Everything else was superfluous. Before my parents went grocery shopping, my siblings and I would run up to put in our chocolate-bar order. If it was during a particularly gripping part of a television program (i.e., Sam and Diane's first kiss, or Sam and Rebecca's first kiss), one was allowed to order by proxy. "Go tell them I want a Caramilk bar," I would order Navjit. "Make that two," someone else would yell when Navjit went up the stairs to relay our choices.

We knew how to play the game; we always sent the cutest delegate, so when Navjit got older, Sumeet was trained to ask for whatever we wanted.

"Okay, Sumeet," we said. "Go upstairs and ask Mom if we can get McDonald's tonight."

"Make sure to ask Mom," we would remind him, knowing we had hit up our dad just days earlier. "And tell her you want it."

"Say, 'Mom, I want McDonald's' and smile," we said, rewriting the script for ensured success. Flattening his hair and tucking his shirt in for optimal four-year-old cuteness, we would send him on his way and listen at the door.

It usually started out perfectly well. "Mom?" he would say, approaching her in the kitchen.

Then a pause before a quickly deflated "Can I have . . ." Running back to us, he would whisper, "What do I want again?"

At first my parents thought they could force us to love eating Indian food three meals a day. Although my parents still ate Indian food for at least 90 percent of their meals, they soon realized that we had different palates. Over the years, they slowly expanded their recipe repertoire, knowing we would sit in front of cold *saag* all night rather than eat it. My mom can make a delicious pizza now, fluffy golden crust and all. But the early incarnations were far from perfect—ketchup stood in place of pizza sauce and the cheese of choice was processed Cheddar singles until we discovered the existence of mozzarella. And they knew we needed to wash it all down with a fizzy sugary bottle of cola. We were two-bottles-a-day past addicted and the mounds of sugar I consumed in my formative years meant I spent too many years of my adult life with the top button of my jeans undone.

When it came to junk food, we were very orderly. We all had to take turns getting it when there was none in the house, biking to the nearby grocery store with a list in hand and a fistful of pooled money.

"It's your turn to go get stuff," we'd say to the designated runner. "Here's the list and don't get the regular chocolate chip cookies. Get the chewy ones or I'll send you back." If you paid for the food yourself, it was yours, but if our parents purchased it, everything was distributed in a very communist-like fashion.

When a fresh bag of chips was opened, we would all pull out a bowl. The bag would be split equally into five bowls. Everybody was given equal opportunity in our quest to raise the national childhood obesity numbers. Chocolate almonds were counted out into people's palms, leftover cake was cut into equal tiny slivers.

Where other girls had a date with hunky Kenny or fun-loving Bill to look forward to on a Friday night, we had an extra-tangy bag of salt-and-vinegar chips. Food was our friend, our entertainment, our reward, and our Friday-night date. My adolescent dependence on snack cakes had followed me into adulthood, and if I wanted to continue in any physical pursuits, I knew I had to continue my very slow-going attempt to get in better shape.

Jaclyn convinced me to attend a noon-hour aerobics class with her one Wednesday. I had not been to the gym in over a month and couldn't think of a reasonable excuse not to go, so I decided this would be a great jump start to my afternoon. The longer I felt unready to don a bathing suit, the longer it would be before I could start to swim.

Standing outside of the class, I smiled at my-soon-to-be fellow aerobicizers as I adjusted my T-shirt strategically over my love handles. To my horror, some of my coworkers were in the fitness flock.

We smiled politely at one another and flooded into the room when the doors opened. I ran instantly for the back corner, out of view. When I turned back, I saw Jaclyn, dead center and directly in front of two male coworkers. She motioned to the mat beside her and I reluctantly shuffled over. When everyone started grabbing barbells and loading them with weights that would challenge Mr. T, I realized I was in way over my head.

I contemplated making a run for it when the instructor breezed past me, her biceps larger than my buttocks. Her abs rippled as she leaped up onto the platform and screamed, "Are you ready for this?!"

Everyone shouted their affirmative replies and clapped excitedly, drowning out my scream of "No! Not really!"

With a push of a button, "Pump Up the Jam" blasted from the speakers and the instructor motioned for us to pick up our barbells. Jaclyn had loaded mine with what she felt was a good weight for a beginner but felt more like the body weight of a baby elephant.

I struggled to lift the weight and position it on my shoulders as instructed.

"Okay!" the instructor yelled, "Let's squat a superset!"

We squatted once, twice, thrice, again; a superset seemed to be some sort of infinite exercise torture. From this we lunged, then squatted again, and returned to lunging. I looked up at the clock for mercy, but we were only ten minutes into the hour.

"Nice work, everyone!" She-Ra bellowed from the podium. "Now put down the barbells and load on about double the weight for our back segment."

I mimed adding more weight and used the pause for an opportunity to drink half of my water bottle and splash the other half on my face. The chest-and-back set was more torturous than the leg exercises. For most of it, as we lay on the benches to do our chest workout, I threw down my barbells and just punched my fists up in the air.

As my muscles knotted like pretzels, I imagined each blow landing on Jaclyn, who I had believed to be my friend but who had obviously signed me up for a hidden-camera prank. As we moved on to the arm portion of the class, my perspiration had hit epic proportions. My hair was drenched and the only thing that stopped me from wringing it out onto my mat was the intense burning pain in what is apparently called a tricep.

"Almost done," the instructor yelled. Fifteen minutes left. These would be the longest fifteen minutes of my life, second only to the time a boy in my drama class performed a "Vagina Monologue" for his end-of-the-year exam.

I spent the abs section lying on my mat with my eyes closed and the end of the class agonizing through the cooldown.

When I got up from the stretch, my right leg buckled beneath me. Jaclyn put my mat and weights away while I held on to the wall for support and staggered to the change room.

I almost pulled down the shower curtain, grabbing onto it for support. I may have put my dress back on inside out and I cannot verify whose underwear I grabbed from the locker, but I made it back to work, muscles on fire. The next four days I screamed every time I went up and down a stair.

But, despite being embarrassingly out of shape and having two left tap shoes, after three weeks of instruction, I could almost, almost, almost dance. After one week where my instructor had to single me out to help me learn a step, I decided I had to take matters into my own hands. With the blessing of my kindly neighbors below me, I strapped on my tap shoes, turned on some music, and ran through some steps in my living room. I would look up videos on the Internet and practice along the night before each class.

"What's that music you're dancing to?" Navjit asked one night when she came over to watch *True Blood*.

"Um, it's Lil Wayne," I mumbled. "I couldn't find anything else."

"Show me your routine," she said, sitting down. This is when I realized I didn't know the names of any of the steps, only how they looked in the mirror.

"This is called a scuttlebug," I lied, kicking my leg out and tapping the other. "And, um, this is the one-legged jimmy." I leaped into the air and made tapping sounds when I landed.

"Um . . . that's great," she said. We both knew I was lying, but neither of us was going to say anything.

"I need a bit more practice," I said.

. . .

After class one night, I sprinted to the streetcar with a fellow tapper named Sue as the Toronto snow swirled violently around us. Dodging an icy patch on the sidewalk, she asked me what brought me to the class. At first I hesitated. I didn't want to open the can of worms that was my life. It would have been simplest to just say that I loved dance or that I was trying to get into shape. But if I was committed to my project, I had to be open about it.

"Well," I said, a puff of breath freezing in the air over my face, "it's a long story." I told her of my desire to make up for lost time and my plan for the year. Having started on the topic, I asked Sue about the lessons of her youth and she laughed and said, "Well, with Asian parents, I had to take piano. So maybe in a way you were lucky?" I really wasn't sure.

I also wasn't sure if and when I would ever get to Disney World. All I knew was that I had to go. There is an episode of *The Golden Girls* where Dorothy asks her mother, Sophia, where she wants to go on their vacation. Sophia doesn't hesitate to choose Disney World. If Sophia could wait until eighty-four to go, riding Space Mountain with her wicker purse in her hand, I was going to have a blast.

I thought it would be quite hard to convince my fellow adults to come with me on my pilgrimage to Orlando, Florida. But anyone who heard my plan was instantly on board. One friend even devised a plan to drive there—until learning it took twenty-two hours.

My new life resolution had experienced some bumps, but altogether, it was coming along nicely. I had some Disney

World brochures, about a hundred bookmarks saved on my computer for dog breeders and pet adoption agencies, two tap routines half mastered, and I had visited the gym about ten times in the month in preparation for my self-inflicted bathing-suit season. More importantly, I was having more fun than I could have imagined. Instead of continuing to hit SNOOZE on my alarm clock until 8:59 every morning, I got up on time to pack my dance outfit and shoes for the evening class. I had a trip to look forward to and my cellulite didn't believe me, but I actually liked working out. It turned out that creating the life you wanted was infinitely more fun than going through the motions. Why didn't I listen to Dr. Phil earlier?

I was definitely making headway, but with everything I wanted to achieve, I knew that I really had to kick it into high gear to get my goals achieved for the year.

→ SIX ←

sleepover club

The February blahs hit around midmonth, and I began to lose momentum. Like most grown-ups, after a long day at a job that was becoming increasingly stressful, the last thing that appealed to me was adding more to my plate. I had tried to bring healthier meals to work since starting dance class, but when I would get back from a meeting and see a hundred e-mails in my inbox, only a handful of chocolate almonds from my candy drawer were going to suffice. My attendance at the gym was becoming spotty and I was falling back into the trap of thinking exercise was a luxury, not a necessity. I had any and all excuses in the book: I was too tired. I didn't have time to wash my hair at the gym. The cashier begged me to buy at least three boxes of the discount Valentine's Day chocolates.

The truth was that nothing appealed to me more than sitting on my sofa and watching TV, and I was getting more off track than the flight from *Lost*.

So when my lady friends from high school proposed a March weekend in the country, I relished the opportunity to kick-start my resolutions by accomplishing another childhood wish. It wasn't grand enough to require addition to the list, but it would help get me back on track. And I would finally get to attend a rite of passage in girlhood: I was going to a sleepover.

The only times we Gills ever slept over anywhere was when we went to visit relatives or family friends. Then the kids would be relegated to sleep in one room together, whether they wanted to or not. Gurpreet and I once had to sleep with a cousin who gave us head lice, which made me see both the merits of one's own bed and the importance of medical disclosure among children.

I had never been to a real sleepover but imagined it to be the type of experience that would result in buying those dime-store "Best Friends Forever" necklaces that break in half. Deep dark secrets would be revealed and cotton candy would be consumed before everyone drifted off to a tranquil slumber. It meant that you belonged and that you had friends who liked you enough to want to spend eighteen consecutive hours with you. For a child who desperately wanted to be invited to an event, yet knew she could never attend, this was vital validation for me. However, my parents pictured sleepovers as Roman orgies where the sleeping bags were filled with fluffy mounds of cocaine, so my siblings and I were never allowed to attend them growing up.

I asked Jen what a good sleepover required so I could get a kit together. She gave me the list of required sleepover activities, including prank calls, calling boys you like, eating junk food, having a dance party, watching horror films, staying up all night, and doing each other's makeup. Board games and Ouija boards were optional.

There was so much I didn't know, like the importance of "finding a good piece of carpet," as Jen put it, to stake your claim in the hierarchy of the group. "If you're on the outside, then you're not as popular," Jen told me. "It means that nobody wants to sleep beside you." Luckily our sleepover would not involve a piece of carpet—I was thirty and not camping out for Rolling Stones tickets, so would not be going within fifty feet of a musty sleeping bag. Also, we were missing a very integral part of the sleepover: the girls-only invite list.

From what I knew (from episodes of *Beverly Hills, 90210*), the proper role of boys in a sleepover was to peek into your windows or be substituted for by throw pillows that Andrea Zuckerman used to practice kissing. They were not, under any circumstances, to attend. But adult life is different, and being in a relationship means that your significant other can also become your permanent plus one. In fact, the majority of our group was going to consist of couples, save for me, Jess (whose husband was out of town), and Jill's female dog, Cindy (who no doubt would think herself too good to participate in the makeup portion of the night).

I didn't want to be too pushy with my agenda, so I would have to feel out the situation and see if any of the husbands looked as if he wanted to paint his nails and talk about Jordan Catalano from *My So-Called Life*. As watching horror films and eating junk food was not a girls-only activity, I hoped we would still partake in some slumber-party-related activities.

I drove up with Jill, with her dog, Cindy, snuggled in my lap. Jill's boyfriend, Rob, also came up, with his family bulldog, Toby, in tow. "So, what's new?" I asked Jill. It was a three-hour drive to our destination and we hadn't seen each other in months, so it would be a great chance to catch up. Jill started telling me about her decorating plans for her new house and I oohed and aahed at her descriptions of brocade curtains and tufted headboards. Twenty minutes into our three-hour car ride, Rob was sound asleep in the backseat. If our girl talk had already put him to sleep, then he was in for a weekend-long hibernation when we connected with the rest of our gal pals.

Ripping open a bag of chips, we turned on the radio and settled in for a lovely country drive. We sang along to eighties rock ballads on the radio and looked at each other, laughing. Then we looked at each other again. Then Jill looked at Cindy and I looked at the bottom of my shoes. "What IS that?" I screamed.

Toby looked sheepishly out the window. Then she unleashed the foulest scent this side of a Calcutta outhouse in August. We rolled down the windows, frantic. "Wake up!" we screamed at Rob. "Wake up! Wake up!" He laughed, like a mother who was used to the smell of her baby's dirty diapers and didn't understand the commotion.

"Toby just ate something weird," Rob explained. "Don't worry about it."

We kept the windows down for a few minutes before

recalling that it was still the dead of winter. Poor Cindy was shivering, so we were forced to cage ourselves back in and hope for the best.

I looked back at Toby, who was now also asleep. We turned the radio down because as everyone knows, you should let sleeping dogs lie. And you should let dogs that can re-create the scents of Chernobyl sleep indefinitely. But Toby, with her bulldog resilience, was not going to let a small detail like unconsciousness get in the way of her stomach-acid output.

"Oh God!" we screamed, pumping the window levers. "I can't breathe!" I screamed, shoving my head out the window.

Jill alternated driving with her breath held with quick bursts out the window to inhale.

"I don't know if I can make it," I said to Jill, my breath labored.

When we finally reached the country house, I fell out of the car, gasping for air like a deep-sea diver racing for the ocean surface after a shark knocked the tank off his back. We told everyone at the house about our drive and they assumed we were exaggerating. But throughout the two days, Toby made sure to prove our point every half hour or so. "Dear Lord!" someone would scream, knocking over the Scrabble board to find shelter from the smell. "Toby!" someone else would scream from inside the shower.

Watching Cindy and Toby play, I was acutely aware of how easily pets become the focal point of a room. Jill and Rob would wake up at ungodly hours to take the dogs out. Then, as the rest of us sat by the roaring fire, they would pull on their parkas and go out again in the evening. Dogs are wonderful because they always love you, but they also always *need* you.

They don't grow up and get potty-trained, and they won't go off to college and learn to support themselves. I wasn't sure I wanted to be that needed.

Despite fear of methane poisoning, the weekend was fun—jaunts through the village, walks on the winter-swept beach, and games around the fire. But there are certain things that are no longer options when men are involved. Candid conversations, for instance.

"Quite the snowy day out there, huh?" Husband One would venture as we all sat in silence.

"Yes indeed," Gal Pal One would respond. "Really coming down out there, really coming down."

Silence.

"Anyone see that miniature village on the way in?" Gal Pal Three would venture.

"Oh yes, it was great," Husband Two would agree. "We should go back and check that out tomorrow; it looked really interesting."

Silence.

"So," Husband One would say. "Anyone hear the new Nickelback album?"

Dead silence.

When my high school girlfriends and I get together, the majority of our time together is spent talking about high school, men, recipes, our hopes and dreams, and general nonsense. There were times during the weekend when we would all be sitting around talking and suddenly realize that the conversation had taken a distinct turn.

"That's a great bedroom," Jill would say, motioning to the design show currently playing on HGTV.

"That's exactly the type of window treatment I was thinking of doing in my guest bedroom," Stacey said. "Do you think that could work?"

"You probably need a Philips Cobalt 200 drill to get the curtain rod hung perfectly," Rob interjected.

This sparked a heated debate regarding the proper drill bits, whether or not a drywall plug was required, and how to properly change the electrical outlet beside the window to get it up to code. This was not how things happened at the sleepovers in *The Baby-Sitters Club.*

Because of the presence of the gentlemen, I also had to tone down my enthusiasm for all things sleepover-related.

"Who brought the Twister?" I heard someone say shortly after we arrived, while I put away my clothes in the room Jess and I were sharing.

"Oh, ha ha," I said, running into the living room. "What's that doing in there?" Three mud masks tumbled out of the box and I scrambled to pick them up before anybody noticed. "Here, let me take that from you," I said, laughing.

It had taken only two hours and I was already poised to be the girl whose piece of carpet was going to be in the furnace room.

"So what should we do?" Stacey, our gracious host, asked.

"Well," I said, "has anyone seen *The Omen*? *Rosemary's Baby*? *The Fog*? I just happen to have them in my—"

"Let's play Trivial Pursuit," someone said. Fine, Trivial Pursuit it was. No worries, I assured myself. The game will go a couple of hours and then it will only be 11 P.M. In sleepover time, that was close to 7 P.M.

The game ended at midnight. We were asleep at 12:05.

The next day consisted of the very fun but entirely un-sleepover activity of antiquing followed by more board games.

As a traditional kids' sleepover, the weekend was an utter failure. My horror movies lay patiently in my overnight bag and nary a prank call was made. A dance party would have been wholly out of the question and a bra freezing would have been simply humiliating. But as a fun adult getaway, I was having a blast. With the exception of attempting to apply a mud mask to Cindy, I gave up trying to push my agenda on everyone and just enjoyed my weekend out of the city.

When I got to work Monday morning, Jaclyn asked me about the weekend, and when I told her about Toby, she topped my story with the most horrific dog tale ever. In case the reader is eating cereal, as I was when I heard this disgusting tale, I will offer only the broad strokes. Jaclyn's dog, Tucker, had been sick. Like any cute little dog that runs its household, he sleeps in the bed, and on Saturday morning, instead of waking up and smelling the coffee, Jaclyn awoke to the smell of dog crap. Which was running down her pillow. It was across her duvet, on the floor, and under the bed. It was, in short, a shit storm.

After that story and the weekend with Toby, I was now torn on the dog issue. Every dog owner I know says getting a dog was the best move they ever made, one that they would make again without regrets. But being in Toby's line of fire, recalling how Jill set her schedule around Cindy's needs, and the cripplingly disgusting thought of dog diarrhea in my bed made me wonder if a dog and I could share the same lifestyle.

I could admit that none of the real responsibilities of owning a dog crept into my mind the countless times I had begged my parents for one. As an adult, I was finally looking at the question with the rationality my parents would have applied when they broke our hearts time and time again. There's really nothing I hate more than admitting that my parents may have been right.

→ SEVEN ←

tennis the menace

By mid-March, my tap-class term was over and I couldn't believe I had only been dancing for two months. We actually put a short routine together, and though it wouldn't have made the class hunk lean on my locker if I'd performed it at the junior high talent show, I was definitely dancing. More importantly, I found myself looking forward to class every week. Work was becoming robotic and hectic all at once, and having a creative outlet into which I could channel my energy was a great feeling.

Investing in myself was also a great feeling. This was the first class for pleasure I had ever taken and it was rewarding to learn a new skill at an age when people often put learning behind them in the pursuit of earning money.

I wondered if I would be a different person today if I had

done something like it as a kid. I could see myself being more confident and more purposeful. Maybe I wouldn't have started dieting at thirteen or wearing glasses at fourteen, because instead of sitting in front of the TV eating brownies, I would have had something to look forward to one hour a week, the way I did now. I know that a major reason my parents didn't let us take lessons was that they were expensive. On two factory workers' salaries, my parents saved, put a roof over our heads, and gave us the basics, but they didn't believe in indulging in luxuries, for us or for them. My mom has the same work shirts in her closet that I folded when I was eleven years old. They lived life unselfishly, and I was aware that I had a much more self-centered existence.

I admired my parents for it, but I also wish they had let us kids just indulge, once or twice, because I would have loved to have felt as great as I did now, when I was a kid. At first I had been embarrassed to change into my sweats in the work washroom and to see people peep into the class through the studio window, but now I was grateful for that hour a week when I just allowed myself to have the experience of feeling like a kid again.

Though I could only recall the name of half of the steps, I could shuffle, ball-change, and stomp my way through an hour each week. As the class was nearing its end, the majority of the members decided that we would continue on. Our instructor told us he could change the time of the new beginners' class so we could stay in the same time slot and progress in our dancing until we were ready for chorus roles in *Stomp*.

Arriving at class the first day of our new session, I peered into our studio and noticed that it was quite full.

"Is that the tap class?" I asked the girl at the front desk.

"Yes," she told me. "We're combining your class with the new beginners' class."

This didn't sound that good to me. Instead of paying for the whole term, I decided to test the waters and paid only for that class.

When I walked in, I saw four of my classmates to the right and four new students to the left. The new students consisted of one girl in lacy leggings and matching headband, one woman who was already perspiring heavily in her ill-advised tap outfit of polyester pants and a wool turtleneck sweater, and two middle-aged Asian men, one of whom was dressed in cotton Dockers and a button-down shirt tucked into said Dockers. Our half of the class glared over at the beginners. We felt arrogantly superior with our seven weeks of experience in the art of dance. Look at their stances, how amateur. Oh, how they muddled through the shuffle.

Our teachers split the class into two sections, and while the beginner class was taught to do a basic tap-and-step, we were jumping, hopping, and trotting our way through the Shim Sham. Sharing the space was difficult. The beginners tried to keep up with us, while we stood for half of the class watching a tap-instruction déjà vu. To add to my frustration, the turtleneck-wearing woman beside me, now sweating from every visible pore, was tapping along with our "advanced" class. What the hell was she doing? I thought. She kept dancing, crowding the space I needed to "find my inner funk," as my instructor always encouraged.

In addition to this, I was dealing with a situation at work that required me to furiously tap away at my BlackBerry in between buffaloes. At the end of the class, I had learned almost nothing because of these distractions, and during the next class I found myself behind. The class after that, I had two left tap shoes and was given the news that the class would move to 5 P.M. Running out of meetings early because I had tap class was not going to fly at my workplace, so I feared I had done my last ball change.

When I began my quest, I knew that I would take to some experiences more than others, and like a child trying out a variety of after-school activities, I wanted to make it an organic process. If I liked something, I would stick with it. If I hated it, I would move on, but I had to stick with everything long enough to constitute an honest try and attain some minor proficiency. I wasn't going to get a role in *Lord of the Dance* anytime soon, but I could tap the basics. I hoped to find another class in the future, but for the time being, I hung up my tap shoes and returned to my to-do scroll. It was time to check off some boxes.

Luckily, my mind soon became occupied with a new opportunity. When my friend Ilana mentioned that she was going to sign up for tennis lessons, I didn't hesitate to join her. When I was younger, I was obsessed with tennis. My sisters and I loved watching the childish antics of Boris "Boom Boom" Becker and the infamous tantrums of John McEnroe. We watched every match that was on and played whenever we could. By "played," I mean that we hit tennis balls on the street right in front of our house, two sisters playing while the other two acted as ball girls and Pepsi holders.

When I was fourteen, our cousins came to visit from the UK. We hadn't seen them since we were all toddlers, so had no idea what to expect. The four of us dressed up in our *salwaar kameezes* and flashed them big (in my case metal-mouthed) smiles when they came to our door. They greeted us with a traditional *sat-sri-akal* and we reciprocated and awkwardly perched on chairs as they talked in Punjabi with our parents about all the family goings-on.

"What do you think?" Gurpreet asked when we were alone in the kitchen.

"They seem kind of shy," I said.

After a few days of us all exchanging pleasantries, talking about such exciting topics as the average rainfall in Cornwall, and feigning interest in *Coronation Street,* Gurpreet had the best idea since sliced naan.

"Should we play tennis outside?" she said. Those five words completely changed our summer, as it turned out that four cheap hardware-store racquets were all we needed to break the ice between us and our visitors.

"We thought you lot were gonna be so boring," one of our cousins told us one night as we all laughed about our first impressions. "Why were you wearing suits?"

We ended up having a very fun visit. For me and my sisters, it was the first summer in memory that we were outside more than we were in the basement. Not only were we *encouraged* to socialize, if we didn't we would be in trouble with our parents for being bad hosts. We played tennis at least five times a week, holding full-out continental tournaments that would last well into the evening hours, pausing only for pizza delivery and passing cars. It was like we were starring in a

Bollywood film set at a tennis camp in the hills of Shimla. All that was missing was a five-hour song-and-dance sequence modeled on a Janet Jackson video from the previous decade.

The next year, when Gurpreet and I went to visit our cousins in England, we packed our tennis racquets as if we were heading to Wimbledon. One day our uncle took us all to visit Warwick Castle, and we brought the racquets along, hearing that the adjoining park had courts. While our uncle tried to entice us with the castle's more interesting features (dungeon chambers and the gift shop) our hands itched for the soft supple leather (more likely vinyl) of a racquet's handle. Once our tour was finished, we ran across the grass to the tennis courts and began the tournament of champions. We played for hours, my uncle patiently waiting by the gate, until the castle grounds grew dark and we finally called it a game. I can't recall who won, so I'll just assume it was me.

After that summer, I returned to school and decided I would try out for the tennis team. After months of concerted practice, this was my best chance to get on a school sports team.

"I think I might try out for tennis," I said to Melodie, who was on almost every team the school offered.

"Oh, do it!" she said. "We could have so much fun at practice and we could do doubles in the tournaments."

"Okay," I said, excited by the possibility. "I think I will."

"I didn't actually know you played tennis," she said.

"Well, I just started last year," I said. "But I played the whole summer."

"I bet you're awesome," she said. "Don't slaughter me in the tryouts!"

I didn't know if I was awesome, but after several unsuccessful years of trying out for basketball, then volleyball, then track, then badminton, I thought I finally had a shot. Arriving at the tryouts, I took my place on the court and faced off against my first opponent. She was two years younger and half a foot shorter, so I made a mental note to take it easy on her. Nobody likes a show-off.

As she readied herself to serve, I bent my knees, steadied my gaze, and conjured up an image of my seamless return forehand.

Her first serve shot right past me in a blur. The second nearly broke my racquet, and the third nearly broke my shinbone.

When my serve hit the net, she yelled, "Fault!"

I realized that instead of just playing all summer, I should have watched some tennis too, as my cousins and I didn't play by official rules. We didn't call faults. By our rules, you were allowed two do-overs if you promised to treat your opponent to ice cream after.

After five straight misses in a row, I managed to return her bullet of a volley, and cheered when it coasted right past her.

"Yes!" I said, celebrating my only point of the set.

"That bounced twice on your side," she informed me.

"Aren't you allowed to still hit it if you do a cool trick shot?" I said.

"No," she said. "Where did you make that up?"

I wasn't even going to ask her about the standing rule of having your hand count as another racquet or the rule where if you caught a serve in your hand, it was your choice to bounce it once and return it, or serve yourself. I had been playing by Punjabi rules for way too long and didn't know the singles line from the doubles line. All I knew was that I was getting my ass kicked.

My opponent polished the court with me. My next opponent also made quick work of me. I had a glimmer of hope when my third opponent dropped her glasses, but her eyes seemed to regenerate after my two double faults. And with that, my tennis-team tenure was over.

"How did it go?" Melodie asked me after finishing her tryout with a second group on another court.

"Maybe I need to take a break from tennis," I said.

I officially ended that break when Ilana and I walked into the high school gymnasium that would house our tennis class. I was hit with the memories of matches past, along with the smell of chalk mingled with body odor. The class looked like a microcosm of high school. There were the pretty blondes, the nerds, the unnoticed mass, the gung ho types, and the mature students. And by "mature," I don't mean that they failed math and came back for their senior year. I mean that they were senior citizens.

"Nobody played like Arthur Ashe," one of the women stated. "Absolutely nobody." We all nodded silently lest she begin a debate about it. Another woman informed our instructor that she had to miss a class due to a bingo tournament.

Our instructor, a middle-aged man who didn't feel it was necessary to give his name, put us through the drills for an hour, which would have been grueling if three-quarters of our time wasn't spent lined up against the wall, waiting for our chance at the net. We stood in the line for ten minutes, had a shot at hitting one ball, then fell back into the line. Five minutes into the class, a ball careened off a basketball net and hit me square in the head. Though it hurt like a BB-gun blast, I laughed it off while one of the pretty blondes giggled and apologized. I would have planned a subtle revenge but I was well aware that my lack of ball control would have made that impossible. Attempting a crafty lob to her back would no doubt result in a ball stuck in the roof instead.

Still, tennis was undoubtedly my favorite activity thus far. Everyone in my class was incredibly friendly and I discovered that I was actually half decent. Only 60 percent of my shots bounced off the ceiling, which was better than the class average. After only one class, I was dedicated to tennis. I persuaded anyone who was free to help me practice on the weekend and borrowed racquets for those who didn't have one but were willing to donate their time. I dreamed of actually being able to play a match. I was a long way off but it was a nice possibility. The great thing about tennis was that it was not just a skill but a social activity; nobody ever suggested meeting a friend to tap-dance together. Perhaps Gregory Hines did, but that is not a fact I can prove.

As spring progressed, Navjit started to join me on the public courts to help me practice. She was a beginner as well but played with gusto.

"Another game for Milos!" she would scream every time she got a ball past me, imitating an Eastern European tennis pro from an episode of *Seinfeld*.

"It was out!" I said.

"No need to get caught up in details," she countered.

Tennis was giving me a chance to spend more time with Navjit, which our schedules rarely allowed. But whenever or wherever I wanted to play, I knew I could count on Navjit to come and help me practice and say things like "Good hustle, buddy" even when I missed the shot.

The thought of one day playing a real game was exciting to me. It offered the opportunity to move from new skill to new social activity. It was a concrete and tangible goal but it needed more attention than a once-a-week lesson, so I booked private lessons for a real kick start. Every Tuesday after work, I would change in the washroom and lug my work clothes and tennis bag down to a court to get one-on-one attention, and entertain passersby as my instructor yelled "Hit it OVER the net!" at me. I was definitely improving, but those improvements were sometimes invisible to the naked eye. But my tally of activities was growing. I could now tap, my tennis skills were improving, and with the newfound confidence I had from those achievements, I decided I had to add something else to the list.

→ EIGHT ←

driving miss desi

My new activities were really buoying up my self-esteem, so I decided I had to channel that energy into another activity that had haunted me since the age of sixteen: driving. The problem was that I really hated it. As a kid growing up in a strict house, I dreamed of freedom, and yet here I was, depriving myself of it in some measure as an adult. The last few months had shown me the satisfaction attached to going back and tying up lost threads from the past. My self-esteem had increased exponentially with each tap step I mastered and forehand I hit, so I wanted to ride that upward momentum and tackle my biggest regret from my teenage years.

Part of the reason I didn't drive as a teen was that it offered me a much better excuse for why I couldn't go out than a cousin's birthday. How could I go somewhere if I couldn't get there? "I wouldn't want to put you out," I would say to those who would offer to pick me up. "Besides, I'd have to leave early because I have [insert excuse here] in the morning."

Funnily enough, my parents wanted us kids to drive. They didn't want to give us the car so we could go places, but they felt we should have the skill. There were too many little kids to chauffeur, and the more chauffeurs, the better. They also didn't get why I was so hesitant about learning. They told me I should practice but I didn't want to have to practice with them. They were both decent drivers, despite the "tender fender" my mom had been in a few years back, which my dad liked to remind her of. One day when she and I went to the store, which she forced me to do, because there was a limit of four milk bags per customer at the sale price, while I was closing the trunk, I looked into the car to see her sitting in the passenger seat. "You drive," she said.

It was only two streets to get home, so I just drove the car while she sat silently. Driving with my dad, on the other hand, was an altogether different undertaking. A conversation with my dad is more like going to a university lecture than a two-sided discussion. You could either nod along or take notes in a steno pad as he offered you a fifteen-minute dissertation on a variety of topics from his theories on U.S.-Russian relations to his ideas about more sustainable energy sources. This was, of course, very distracting when you were driving, especially for a new driver.

"Maybe we could talk about Henry Kissinger later," I would say, trying to negotiate a left turn. He would be silent for a minute then remember a great joke he had heard on his Indian radio channel.

"Oh, this is funny . . . a Sikh man, a Hindu, and a goat go into . . ."

It would be at that point that I would drive too close to the yellow line and he would lose his humor and lecture me the whole rest of the way home.

Despite my desire to finally get behind the wheel again, I heard myself already making excuses. "It's winter," I would say to one friend. "Wow, the price of gas is really ruining my driving plans!" I would lie to another. While I was out shopping one day in April with Jen, she asked me if I wanted to pump gas and I shook my head furiously and buckled my seat belt. I don't know why I am so afraid of all things vehicular. It seemed that as each year passed, I had a little more trepidation. Much like not knowing how to swim, or learning new skills, not having confidence was a thing I wanted to leave behind in childhood memories. I realized how stupid I was being and got out of the car.

After pumping the gas and realizing a monkey could do it, I decided I would have to take driving in small steps. But I couldn't allow myself to keep putting it off. Relying on someone to chauffeur me around was not freedom. I wanted to go antiquing, take weekend trips, drive my eventual brood of adorable wide-eyed kids to the zoo, and take road trips across this great continent of ours, and all that was standing in my way was my fear.

My friend Moira offered to take me driving. Others had

offered from time to time but found themselves having to wash their hair when I reminded them of it. In fairness, though, it was a subject that I rarely brought up. I had avoided driving for the past decade, and despite my putting it on the top of my must-do list, old habits were dying hard. So I made a date with Moira and didn't let myself back out of it, no matter how desperately I wanted to wash my hair.

My issue was pure and simple: a complete lack of confidence. Had I started driving at sixteen like everyone else I knew, I would have had three years of steady driving experience before heading off to college, but I had resisted. It was the summer after my first year of university that I decided to finally take driving lessons. I was back at home and working two jobs, so I thought I'd add salt to the wounds of my already terrible summer and learn to drive. It was no surprise to me when my parents bypassed the large and reputable companies to sign me up at an Indian driving school.

The advantage to this was that the school allowed me to skip the in-class lessons, for which I had no time. My instructor was the calmest human I had ever encountered; Gandhi was teaching me how to parallel-park.

We would drive for an hour a week, and during that hour, he would tell me where to turn and advise me of how far I was over or under the speed limit. During the first few lessons, he would remind me of a fundamental by quietly repeating it, saying, "Mirror, mirror, mirror," in a steady chant until I got into the habit of checking them all regularly as I drove. Soon he cut out the verbal cues and simply tapped his finger on the mirrors when he thought I was getting lazy. My eyes darted furtively from one mirror to the other with each tap I heard, like a Pavlovian dog with a learner's permit. The one and only time I drove on the freeway, during my first test, I don't know how I didn't create a ten-car pileup, but somehow I passed with flying colors and moved up to the second level.

My final driving test was scheduled for Thanksgiving weekend and my instructor came to drive me there and offer me a few last-minute tips. When we pulled into the parking lot of the driving test center, he wished me luck and looked in the window to see which test instructors were on duty. "I hope we get the fat one," he said, having acquainted himself with all the testers. Sure enough, a portly lady sidled up to the side of the car and climbed into the passenger seat.

She instructed me to pull out, which I managed to do after she pointed out that my hand brake was on. I feared I had blown it right there but had no choice but to continue. Trying to calm my nerves, I attempted small talk.

"Nice day, isn't it?" I said.

"Mm-hmm . . ." she murmured while furiously scribbling on her notepad.

"Have you done many tests today?" I said sweetly, hoping my interest in her line of work would help win her favor.

"Too many bad ones," she snorted.

"Oh, ha ha." I laughed.

Her tone made me positive that she was already counting mine among them, so I gave up on the pleasantries. I drove where she told me to, turned at her request, and three-point-turned at her heart's desire.

When we pulled back into the lot, I saw my dad out of the corner of my eye and anticipated his response to what I was sure was my failure. He had a way of really seeking out the negative in a situation. His idea of being realistic was to keep the glass perpetually half empty, even if he ended up tipping some water out himself. I knew he was going to point out everything he felt I did wrong, like a football coach reviewing the tapes of the team's losing game, then recount those failures to anyone who would listen. I was aware that I had done badly and didn't need this extra hammering to my self-esteem to drive that point home.

"Okay," the instructor said. "Congratulations."

Her tone was so curt that it took a minute for her words to register. I beamed as I joined the ranks of the full-fledged drivers, and not even the drive home, during which I took my usual position in the passenger seat and listened to my father relaying his utter surprise that I hadn't failed, was going to bring me down.

Ten years later, standing on the porch waiting for Moira, I hoped to recapture that triumphant feeling, but realized that I had not driven in at least five years. And I had never driven in Toronto, city of blaring horns and drivers with loose interpretations of stop signs. Climbing into the passenger seat, I wondered what I was thinking. Not only was I unprepared, but Moira had only received her full license a year prior. In that time, she bought herself a Volkswagen and commuted to work daily and even once drove into Manhattan from Hartford, Connecticut. I admired her confidence, but I also recalled driving with her, my hand gripping the dashboard while she slammed on her brakes at stop signs or sped through the city at ungodly speeds. She wasn't a bad driver, but she sometimes drove like a teenager, complete with Britney Spears sound track and desire to answer every text message she heard ding, in case it was from a cute boy.

Perhaps I should have waited for a veteran who could help me maneuver out of a ditch or plan my best escape route after sideswiping the mirrors off a row of parked cars. But at the rate I was going, that would schedule my return to the road to coincide with my retirement. So I decided to seize the opportunity and give it a shot.

We drove up to a nearby quiet area, which also happened to be one of the most expensive neighborhoods in the city. It offered a new driver the comfort of little traffic mixed with the anxiety of driving past rows of luxury cars. Behind the wheel, I didn't feel as nervous as I thought I would but couldn't say the same for Moira.

Moira rarely frowned. When she was awake, she was all smiles. I mention the disclaimer of wakefulness because her claim to fame was her ability to fall asleep anywhere and everywhere. It was like making plans with Rip Van Winkle. After fifteen minutes of waiting impatiently on a street corner, you would call her for an explanation and hear, "I don't know what happened, I fell asleep!" Making dinner plans often involved working around her nap schedule, and one memorable day, she called to cancel our dinner date because she had eaten some gnocchi at lunch that had induced a pasta coma. On this day she managed to stay awake while I was driving, but her trademark smile was soon replaced with a look similar to the one on Mia Farrow's face during the majority of *Rosemary's Baby*.

"How am I doing?" I asked Moira as I slowly pulled out of a cul-de-sac.

"Um, you might want to move over," she said through terror-clenched teeth. "You're pretty close to that Mercedes."

"Oh, sorry." I giggled. Still, daredevil that she is, she let me continue. "Am I going too fast?" I asked.

Looking at the speed-limit sign, she said, "No, you're ten under."

"Better to be cautious," I said, hands locked at ten and two. "I don't want to scratch up your car or injure any trophy wives." With the exception of nearly missing one stop sign, I was just as good a driver as any sixteen-year-old out there. I even executed a fairly impressive three-point turn and drove for a full minute on a major thoroughfare. Then Moira, visions of fiery collisions no doubt in her mind, told me to go back to the other neighborhood, where it was quieter.

She instructed me to take a shortcut and I found myself going through a narrow alley, just an inch of space to spare on each side of the car. Stay cool, I told myself. Slow and steady, slow and steady. I pulled my foot off the gas and concentrated on coasting through.

As we emerged on the other side, Moira said, "That was great, you made it over that pothole smoothly."

I was confused and looked in my rearview mirror, where I spotted a pothole almost the width of a car, waiting for its tire prey. I didn't feel the need to tell Moira that I had been unaware of the pothole and that sheer luck had gotten us over it. Letting her think I was an adept driver was better for both of us.

I circled through the streets for another hour, conscious of both the cars on my side and the rich soccer moms impatiently trailing me in their SUVs.

"Go around me!" I would motion, but they never did. Now that Moira felt comfortable, I was worried that she would be lulled to sleep, so we decided to head home. When Moira dropped me off, I felt a sense of accomplishment. I know that driving is not brain surgery, but since I was sixteen, I had let a mountain be created from a molehill and now I was finally on my way to climbing it. It was a great feeling and I visualized my ultimate goal, driving down the highway on the ultimate road trip, a perfect playlist on the stereo and a perfectly confident driver behind the wheel.

I decided to join the local auto share program so I would always have access to a car, and most importantly, some insurance. When the online system lavished its acceptance on me, I beamed and Jen suggested a little afternoon drive of celebration. Which is when the smile died. Though I had driven just the past weekend, I was already nervous again.

"I won't be able to back out of your parking spot," I stammered. "That left turn out of our street is too advanced for me." Nonetheless, we agreed to go for a ride and see how I felt about driving home.

Well, *I* agreed with that.

Jen made a right turn off our street, careened down the next street, and pulled over onto the shoulder. Smiling wickedly, she jumped out of the driver's seat and I had no choice but to trade places with her.

"Fine," I said. "I take no responsibility for passenger-side impact."

She didn't flinch, so I cautiously pulled out onto the street, awaiting her instructions. It was a holiday weekend, so streets that would normally be bumper-to-bumper chaos were virtually empty.

"Okay," Jen said, motioning to two cars a foot ahead of me on a quiet street. "Pull up right beside that first car." When I was in place, she said, "Now parallel-park."

I had no idea how to parallel-park. I wasn't even that proficient in regular parking. I recalled many failed attempts to pull through a spot to the one adjacent and hearing a car horn blare at me. How was I supposed to know they were waiting? And really, aren't the yellow lines just a guide?

"Fine," I said. I took a deep breath and looked into the rearview mirror.

"Sharp right, sharp right, sharp right!" Jen coached. "Now left, left, left."

I jerked the wheel from one side to the other, the car moving a millimeter each time, beads of sweat dripping down my forehead.

"Okay, stop! Stop!" Jen said. I jerked to a stop and turned off the car.

I made it. Not even a bump against the curb.

"Okay," I said, quite pleased with myself. "What next?"

What was next was more parallel parking. Ten more parallel parks. Jen seemed to think that parking upon arrival was more important than learning to drive to the destination. She spouted off a statistic about parking-lot accidents.

I reciprocated with a lie about having to get home to watch a show and she let me off the hook. When I got home, I immediately wished I had stuck it out because I really felt like getting behind the wheel again. I dialed Jen's number and left a message.

"Hi, it's me. When can we do that again?"

→ NINE ←

step by step

I turned thirty-one in May, rather unceremoniously, upon my request. When I was younger, all I wanted was to have a birthday party, to play pin the tail on the donkey with my friends, and give out loot bags. The only kids who were ever at our parties were our cousins. Our ignorance of Western birthday-party etiquette was evident when Gurpreet and I were allowed to go to our next-door neighbor Anita's seventh birthday party at McDonald's.

We were so excited that we kept bothering our mom the whole week to get Anita a gift. We couldn't show up at our only social affair of the year empty-handed. After we twirled around the Grimace bars and went down the Hamburglar slide at our local McDonald's, Anita's parents asked us to gather around so Anita could open her gifts. When she got to ours, I sat in anticipation of the big reveal.

"This is beautiful," Anita's mom said, pulling out the turquoise beaded necklace and matching earrings that we had helped our mom choose. I was beside myself with excitement. We were at a party, we were having fun, and people thought we had given Anita a truly awesome gift.

"Oh, wow," the kids said, in between gulps of a sugary powdered drink.

Not having been to a party before, I wasn't aware that I was supposed to sit silently and let the birthday girl move on to the next gift.

"It was only two dollars!" I yelled out.

Gurpreet was so embarrassed that she made a *Kids Say the Darndest Things* face and pinched my arm.

I lost my fervor for birthdays after I turned twenty-one, the age when you officially cross the line from child to adult. After that, each subsequent birthday felt more like aggravation than celebration. Will people show up for my party? Is everyone having a good time? Is so-and-so coming? I decided to spare myself the gift of heartburn for my thirty-first and keep it a small affair. Moira, Jen, Jaclyn, and our lovely redheaded friend Maggie and I met for dinner at a cozy restaurant downtown. "To thirty-one!" we toasted, hoisting our wineglasses in the air. I was now the oldest of the group, though a lifetime of being yelled at to stay out of the sun helped to make me look younger. A handful of wiry gray hairs were my only informants, but they lurked somewhere around layer three hundred of my hair, allowing me to back-comb them into the abyss with little effort.

"Here's to a great year," we cheered.

"And to many more ahead, just like this one," Jen added.

"What's next for you to do?" Maggie asked me.

"Hmm," I replied, not entirely sure.

"I'm going to keep trying with tennis," I replied, "although I am still not very good at it. I have to drive more . . . and choose a camp . . . and look into a trip to Disney World."

As I rattled off the list, I was aware that at thirty-one, I was already completely different from what I was at thirty, or twenty, or even ten, for that matter. I felt a real sense of hope about what I could achieve, because for the first time in a long time, I was actually doing the positive things I had set out to do. No longer was I stuck in the pattern of making myself grandiose promises and being unsurprised that I didn't keep them, then downgrading them to small promises and being disappointed that I couldn't even achieve those. Now I was experiencing the satisfaction of putting my money where my mouth was, and it was taking my life from routine to rejuvenated.

I was happier. I believed in myself more and I believed that life was worth risk and hard work, because it would all work out. It was meant to work out.

Yet, though I had done so much, I still wanted more. As my friends and I talked about the outstanding items on my list, it became apparent that I was nowhere near finished. Like a student who had wasted her whole term partying and suddenly realized that finals were upon her, I had to start cramming or I was not going to make it to the finish line.

With this uncomfortable proposition in mind, I shoved another extremely comforting forkful of steak into my mouth.

I really had to get planning. I am a nauseating overplanner, a habit acquired from a lifetime of being made to feel unable to make wise decisions. If you are a kid who is only going to go out twice a year, you have to choose those outings with a lot of care. My fear of choosing poorly made me indecisive in all decisions in life. I would stand in a department store for ten minutes debating between two pairs of socks and leave both in the end. In high school, I went to the guidance office every week to sign out the university books so I could have four solid years of contemplation before making a choice. Now, having a full-time job and trying to relive two decades of missed opportunities, I would need to demonstrate a certain amount of forethought and wise scheduling. Almost every single day since starting my to-do list, I have gone online and looked at dog photos and Googled such phrases as "having a dog in an apartment" and "breeds that bark the least."

At least ten times I have looked up driving routes to Orlando, Florida. At least five times I have checked the available dates at every camp in North America from piano camps to fantasy camps to good old-fashioned canoe-and-cabin camp.

"Learn to swim," I typed into my Outlook calendar when I got home from dinner. As I looked up adult swim programs, hoping there might be some hosted in all-female gyms or nunneries, I dreamed of gliding through the water, my two braids no longer a barrier.

A message from Navroop popped up on my computer: "Happy Birthday!"

"Thanks," I typed back.

"I think this is going to be your best year ever," she wrote.

"You know what?" I wrote. "So do I."

⇾ TEN ⇽

dog meets world

I wasn't the only one who was making my childhood dreams come true. Gurpreet helped me tick a goal off my list one month in the summer. She had become smitten with a Norfolk terrier in her neighborhood and contacted his breeder to get one of her very own.

"Should I do it?" she asked us.

"Yeah, do it!" we all said, so we could play with a dog that we could then return.

"I don't know," she said. I encouraged her but understood her hesitation. The puppy was expensive and she would be doing it alone and we had all talked ourselves out of having a dog for years.

When a litter was born, she decided to take the plunge and become the first member of our family to have a pet.

"There's never going to be a perfect time," she said. "Sometimes you just have to do something."

That was pretty much my mantra for the year, so I was very excited, partially because I would be able to test the waters by being a pet aunt. The Gills were FINALLY getting a dog!

The breeder lived an hour and a half out of the city, so Gurpreet, Navjit, and I piled into a car to go visit the newly born litter. After we exited the city, I thought we might as well kill two birds with one stone.

"Pull over," I said to Gurpreet.

"Are you sure?" she asked.

"Yes, pull over." We ran out of the car and exchanged seats on the side of the road. I took the wheel and drove the rest of the way, which was smooth sailing . . . except for one very sharp turn onto a country road where I swerved with the speed and aggression of someone being chased by the Dukes of Hazzard.

"Sorry, sorry, sorry," I said as the tires kicked pebbles into the air. "I should have slowed down."

"It's fine," Gurpreet said. She was so excited about seeing the dogs that I could have driven the whole way wearing a sleep mask over my eyes and she'd never have noticed.

At the house, we were like kids in a candy store, picking up puppies two and three at a time. With two in my hand I would go outside and watch two others playing in a wading pool. Navjit and I handled the puppies while Gurpreet asked the breeder her large list of questions. The breeder would decide which puppy would go to which owner and which would be left to become a new show dog.

"Oh, look at this one," Navjit and I would squeal to each other as one of the puppies did something unspeakably cute. Then we began the photo-shoot portion of the day, where we posed with various pups snuggling up to us. After that we commenced the impatient portion of the visit, where we just stood around feeling bored, hoping Gurpreet's long list of questions was near its completion.

After finally signaling to her that we were perhaps overstaying our welcome, we headed out and I drove back up the country highway toward home.

The next week Gurpreet's new dog arrived at his new home. Auggie (a name similar to one I had added to the name registry, but I let it slide) spent his first few days dragging a blanket around and sitting inside a duffel bag on the floor.

I offered to puppy-sit for Gurpreet one day in order to get a feeling for the demands of being with a newborn dog. Auggie arrived for his day with me and was so excited that he peed right in the hallway upon entry. Fair enough, I thought. I *am* very fun and he wants to mark his territory in case another dog tries to claim me for its own. Then he decided to be cautious and mark the whole living room by peeing four separate times in every corner, and as often as possible, on the legs of my beloved dining table. When he was done with that, he topped it off by pooing right beside the sofa and showing it to me, as if he had brought me a hostessing gift. I held him back as I tried to mop the floor, made more difficult by the fact that riding mops seemed to be his preferred method of transportation.

When I tried to walk him, he stopped to sniff and chase everything or would just sit on the curb to stare at people. If they didn't stop, he would sit in their way and wait for them to notice him.

"Come, Auggie, come," I would say, pulling gently at his leash as he stayed firmly planted. "Come on! Do you want treats?" I said to bribe him.

He wasn't all that motivated, though, as his favorite snack was cigarette butts, and lucky for him, they were laid out on each sidewalk block like a buffet. "Bad boy!" I said as he continued to lunge for garbage to eat. After fishing a cigarette out of his mouth for the tenth time, I took him back inside. He thanked me by spitting something up on my arm. After fighting a teddy bear and barking at the door for twenty minutes, he finally curled up in a ball on my carpet and slept, no doubt to regain his energy for his next bout with the bear.

When Gurpreet came to retrieve him, I was bedraggled.

"How was he?" she said.

My arms quivered from pushing a dog-topped mop around as I handed her the leash.

"Oh, okay," I said. I bid Auggie farewell and invited him back when he could present me with evidence that he had successfully graduated from obedience school.

The toilet-paper ads that show puppies chasing rolls down the hallway of a mansion do not properly convey the reality of life with a puppy. I didn't know if I was ready for it. Navroop would be disappointed to hear that I was now firmly ensconced on the fence. The flames of my lifelong desire were not being stoked by seeing and playing with other people's cute dogs. In reality, the sheer exhaustion that went along with the task had the opposite effect, that of dumping a pile of sand on top of the fire.

And yet there had been so many great moments. As I thought back on the day, it was not the vision of Auggie peeing all over the living room that stuck out, but of him sitting at my feet and looking up at me. When he gazed up at me with his head cocked and eyes full of wonder, I couldn't help but forgive his using my living room as his private restroom.

Everyone in my family was falling madly in love with Auggie. He was the dog we had waited our whole lives for. Whenever my sisters and I spoke, a single subject often dominated the conversations.

"Auggie peed on the paper today," Navjit said. Navjit was a cat lover herself, but she had worked at a vet clinic for years, so was our resident Dog Whisperer.

Unfortunately Auggie didn't seem to care whether someone whispered or yelled, because he had no plans to follow any commands. Although we didn't want to let him become spoiled, it was hard because like Michelle Tanner saying "Cut. It. Out." to Uncle Joey on *Full House,* Auggie seemed to know that his cuteness was going to get him anything he wanted.

Luckily, his cuteness got us something *we* wanted too: my parents were slowly turning into dog people. When Gurpreet brought Auggie to their home, their reaction made us wonder what their issue had been all those years.

"That's a good boy," my dad would say as he passed Auggie in the hall, even if Auggie was only sleeping.

"See?" we said to him. "Dogs aren't that much trouble."

My dad would shrug and walk away. Auggie mainly stared up at my dad, no doubt wondering who the giant man in front of him was. But it was a different story with my mom, as Auggie followed her everywhere.

"Who's in there?" we asked one another as Auggie sat in front of the washroom door.

"Mom's having a shower," someone would answer.

When my mom sat down on the hallway stairs to tie her shoes before leaving for work, Auggie would jump up and wedge himself behind her back.

"See? Dogs are fun," we would say to our mom.

"Yes, he's nice," she would answer, patting him on the head like he was a small child. My parents still didn't want him drooling on the furniture or peeing on the carpet, but their actions spoke louder than the words they wouldn't say: despite always dissuading us from the thought when we were kids, they liked having a dog around.

→ ELEVEN ←

lady and the camp

In the seventh grade, the end-of-the-year trip was to a camp situated on a beautiful lake. It was to last a full week and was the first time in my and my fellow students' academic careers that we had ever been presented with the option of a school-sanctioned co-ed overnight trip. We were alerted of the trip at the first assembly of the year.

"Some of you may have heard of the end-of-the-year camp trip," the principal announced at our opening-day assembly. A buzz of excitement ran through the crowd, while my stomach sank at the battle I would have in persuading my parents to let me go.

"It's a lot of fun and you can fund-raise to help offset part of the cost." Offset costs! My parents liked phrases like that. I leaned forward in my seat to catch the vital information that would get camp closer to my parents' very favorite price of "free."

"In one week," the principal continued, "we'll begin fund-raising. This year we're fund-raising with almond chocolate bars." He held up a chocolate and I leaned forward even farther, in case he was going to throw it out into the crowd, like Steven Tyler did with his scarf at Aerosmith concerts. "The chocolates are three dollars apiece, and for every dollar you raise, you get twenty cents' credit that you can use toward the cost of camp."

The camp was $175 for the week, so at twenty cents a pop, I was going to have to pray that a sumo-wrestling convention came to town so I could raise enough to make a dent in the cost.

"Are you going to camp?" a girl in front of me asked her friends as we filed out of the assembly.

"Oh yeah," her friend answered. "I hear it's the most amazing week ever. My sister said you get to choose who's in your cabin and you swim every day and get to see all the guys in their bathing suits."

This presented a world of problems for me. What if nobody chose me for their cabin? Seven days of swimming meant seven distinct chances to drown, or seven excuses that needed to be made about why I wasn't going into the water. And if we saw the boys in their bathing suits, that meant my ultimate fear, that they would be seeing *me* in *mine,* would be realized.

But still, if people's sisters were still talking about the trip, it must be pretty epic. It could change my boring life in so many ways. There was a chance I would get to bunk with girls who would become my new best friends. We would reunite every summer as adults and recall that fateful trip that brought us together while we planned our annual trek to Lilith Fair. Maybe I would find my long-lost twin sister like the character did in *Parent Trap* and she would teach me all of the cool hairstyles she had learned to camouflage her sideburns. But the most exciting thing was not what could happen, but what I knew couldn't: my parents could NOT run out to the lake every day and yell, "Come in now, you have to vacuum the basement!" I didn't know what was going to happen; the opportunities seemed endless. I just knew that I had two months to fund-raise before the deposit was due and I had to get moving.

"How many boxes?" the secretary asked when I got to the front of the chocolates pickup line.

"I'll take fifty please," I said.

"Fifty?" She laughed. "Most kids take two or three."

"Oh, okay," I said, disappointed. "I guess I'll take three."

I walked home with my three boxes after school. Two were in my knapsack, causing my shoulders to hunch back under the pressure. The other was in my hand, already opened. I thought it wise to sample the merchandise before I took it door-to-door, in case of questions. Now, after eating two of the family-size bars, I felt I was ready to answer any queries from prospective clients.

"How many nuts per bar, you ask? They average from nine to twelve."

Or: "I'm glad you asked that, Mrs. Sanders, this is definitely one of the milkier bars I have tried. I would say creamier than a Hershey, more comparable to a British Dairy Milk." I was going to sell out of bars by week's end.

"Is that chocolate?" Navroop asked when I got home.

"Yes," I said. "But it's to fund-raise for my camp trip, so you have to pay if you want one.

"Mom," I said, spotting my mom in the kitchen. "Can you buy some chocolate bars? Navroop wants some."

"Okay," my mom said. "Give her one."

"Well, I want one too . . ." I said.

"Oh, okay, buy two and share them."

My first two bars had been sold without effort. Really, it was four, because I assumed my parents would cover the cost of my test bars too.

"I'm fund-raising for our class trip," I said to my mom to gauge her reaction.

"Don't eat them all," she cautioned.

When my sisters heard that there was a full carton of chocolate bars in my room, I began steadily moving product. Deals were cut, allowing IOUs until allowances were given, and exchanges were allowed for room cleaning and extra dish-drying shifts.

"Shouldn't you sell them to other people, instead of just us?" my mom asked later that week, when she saw my sisters and me nibbling on another bar while watching *The Hogan Family.*

"I will," I said. "I'll sell them all on the weekend."

When the weekend rolled around, I finally pulled out the remaining two boxes and headed out to court some new sales.

"Hi, Mrs. Clarke," I said when my next-door neighbor answered her door. "Would you like to help me raise money for my class trip by buying some chocolate bars?"

I reached into the box, anticipating that she would want a couple. "Oh no," she said. "Some kids came around here already. One came on Tuesday and another on Thursday and we already bought some."

"Oh," I said, my weeklong sugar high finally wearing off.

"Oh, don't worry," she said. "I'm sure we could use another."

"Thanks," I said, handing her a bar. "If you need more, you know where you can find me."

As I made my way around my street, I cursed myself for not having hit the pavement the very first day.

"Oh, sorry, love," neighbor after neighbor said. "We already bought a bunch."

After two hours of ringing bells, I had sold only six bars.

I went out the next day as well and sold bars to relatives here and there, but many of the chocolates ended up being consumed over the next month by the seller and her three sisters. Of the thirty-six bars I brought home, my parents ended up buying ten for us to eat.

I had raised a grand total of $7.20 toward my goal. Despite the setback, the week that they handed out the camp permission slips, I took one.

"Aren't you excited?" my friend Jen asked me as we looked at the forms in our history class.

"Yeah," I said. "It's gonna be so fun. I just hope I can go, because my cousin is getting married that week."

I knew by this point that there was a chance that I wouldn't be going, so I had to get my excuse ready early.

"Oh, that's too bad," Jen said. "We could be in the same cabin."

I thought about that fun proposition all the way home from school.

"What should I say?" I asked Navroop and Gurpreet as we watched our after-school *Amen* marathon.

"I don't know," Navroop said. "They'll probably say no."

"I didn't go to mine," Gurpreet said. "So I don't know."

Not only did Gurpreet not go, she didn't even ask to go because she was not interested either in singing "Cat's Cradle" around the campfire or in fighting with our parents. She knew what they would say no to (pretty much everything) and didn't press it, in the hopes that they would later remember her forbearance and award her a Daughter of the Year award.

I, on the other hand, knew that winning over the kids in school would be a hundred times easier than ever winning over my parents, and had no choice but to exhaust myself with begging, if it was something I really wanted.

"Okay," I said. "I'll ask them after we eat *roti*."

When my mom called us for dinner, I tucked the permission slip in my pocket and ran down the stairs.

"Should I put out the plates?" I asked my mom, grabbing cutlery from the drawer.

We ate dinner in silence, as we always did, and I was so nervous I thought I might choke on my *paneer*. After dinner, my sisters quickly scattered so as not to be caught in the cross fire of what they knew was coming.

"Dad," I said, when it was just my parents and me in the kitchen, "at the end of the year, they have a camp trip and we can fund-raise cheese in the winter to pay for some of it. If I can help pay for it, can I go?"

He looked at the permission slip I had put in front of him and said, "Forget about it."

"But why?" I pleaded. "Everybody else is going to go."

"Your sister didn't go on hers," my mom said.

"Well, she didn't want to," I said. "I really want to. I'll help pay for it. See, it'll only be a hundred dollars."

"No," my dad said, pushing his chair out and walking away.

"Please, Mom," I said as I helped her clean up.

"Your dad said no," she said.

My parents always said no. We were never allowed to question why. A no was a no and you were supposed to then quash the desire in your heart, nod, and say, "Okay, that seems fair," and bow to acknowledge their wisdom.

I went up to my room and stared at the slip. It was due in one week, and if my parents didn't fill it out, I would spend the rest of the school year listening to kids plan their cabin mates and decide who to sit beside on the bus.

I was relentless all that week, hoping I could break my parents down, and I was also incredibly desperate. Not going to camp would be social suicide for me. Everybody went. If you didn't go, it was for one of two reasons: your parents couldn't afford it or your parents wouldn't let you. I was in the combo category.

"I can get a paper route," I said to my dad the next evening. "Then I can pay for the whole thing."

"I said no," he said. "No."

The next night I put the permission slip up on the fridge

with the due date highlighted. On Thursday night, nearly in tears, I enlisted my sisters' help for a final attack.

"Just let her go," Navroop said.

"I hear it's nice," Gurpreet added. "Lots of teachers supervise," she added, knowing what my parents would want to hear.

"Please, Dad," I said. "I'll never ask for anything again. I promise. If you let me go . . ."

"Enough!" he said. "I already said no. You kids are driving me crazy."

"Okay, okay," my mom said, trying to defuse the situation. "All right, kids. Rupinder, you're not going."

Sometimes it seemed, as I was growing up, that my parents just said no, regardless of whether or not the decision actually meant anything to them. It was just the easiest way. It saved them money, it saved them the worry, and they seemed to think that I and my siblings would easily get over whatever we were denied, and forget that we were ever denied it.

I went up to my room and stayed there the rest of the night, not even coming down when Gurpreet called me to watch a new episode of *The Fresh Prince of Bel-Air.*

"I'm sorry," Navjit said, coming to my room with a stick of her Kit Kat bar.

"Thanks," I said, taking the stick.

I couldn't sleep that night, and lay in bed worrying about how I would be able to get the slip in tomorrow. I set my alarm and had barely slept when it rang at 6 A.M. At six-thirty both my mom and dad would leave for work, so this was my very last opportunity to wear them down. I walked slowly down the stairs, already feeling defeated but determined to give it one last effort. When they saw me walk into the kitchen, they already knew why I had woken up that early.

"I told you once, twice, every time," my dad said in Punjabi. "You are NOT going." I climbed back up the stairs, ripped up the permission slip, and cried until my alarm rang at seven-thirty.

People talked excitedly about camp for the rest of the year, while I tried to tune their discussions out. The week of the trip, I had to choose from a number of other activities the school offered as compensation. I already knew to sign up for the cheapest options, so I drew pictures in the art room, visited a local farm, and toured a miniature village, all the while imagining all my friends bonding and creating memories they would reminisce about for years to come.

Years later, Navjit and then Sumeet managed to persuade my parents to let them attend the very camp I had cried over not attending for a whole week. My parents had somehow come around to the realization that the place wasn't the Manson Family cult lodge they originally thought it to be.

"Why didn't you let me go?" I asked my parents as they signed Navjit's permission slip.

"I don't remember you asking," my dad responded.

My parents had softened a lot as the years went by, realizing the world wasn't the frightening place they had always imagined when we asked to step out into it. But it was still annoying that my dad had taken his own advice and "forgotten about" something that I had thought about every day of seventh grade. Nonetheless, I was sincerely happy that my younger siblings had won that battle, and eighteen years after my first attempt, I was looking far and wide for a camp to finally attend.

This was by far the most difficult of all of the activities on my list to coordinate. Camps for adults do exist, of course, but I wasn't willing to spend five grand to have Slash show me how to rock at a rock-'n-roll fantasy camp and too many of the options were basically Zen-based fat camps.

I spent months trolling for a camp that fit my schedule and desire for an authentic camp experience, but nothing seemed to fit the bill. "This is an unusual request," said the customer-service representative from a science camp I found outside of Montreal.

"Oh yes, I understand," I said, having encountered this response enough times now to anticipate it.

A few camps never responded to my queries, some responded and let me know that they had no space or anything scheduled, and some let me know that I was just plain weird. My usual script sounded something like this: "I'm just looking to have a camp experience. I always wanted to go when I was a kid and didn't, so I thought I'd go now. Do you have any programs for adults?"

"Hmm . . . let's see," the woman from the science camp said. "We have the explorer afternoon, for kids and adults together. You could come to that."

"I don't have a kid," I said.

"Could you borrow one?" she said.

"I think people who borrow kids are called kidnappers," I joked.

She transferred me to her boss.

I gave my same speech and she was sympathetic, but said, "We just couldn't have an adult here with the kids. It would be weird."

After months of researching, reaching out, and rejections, I was officially weird. I had almost given up when an Internet search led me to a volunteer posting for a summer camp run by Gilda's Club. Named after Gilda Radner, Gilda's Club had, for many years, been providing those stricken by cancer with support and various programs. I was familiar with the organization, having volunteered for one of their variety-show fund-raisers. For kids, they offered camps in the summer and over March break, with a variety of activities within the city. The minute I saw the posting I realized that this was what my experience was meant to be. Perhaps my lack of success with finding a camp for myself was karmic; the universe's way of telling me that this was not something that I could go back in time and re-create, but I could most certainly help a group of worthy kids have the chance to experience it.

The camp was to last a full week and started bright and early on a Monday morning in early June. As kids started streaming into the playroom, I was reminded of how long it had been since I was the cyclone of energy known as a child. The kids were between four and eleven. Some had diagnoses of cancer themselves, whereas others were coping with a diagnosis in their family. Gilda's Club provided them with an environment of support and a group that could empathize, but camp was their time to just let loose and be kids.

Most of the other counselors had a lot of camp experience and at least half were studying early childhood education. I knew I would be at a disadvantage unless I found a kid who was fascinated with the intricacies of press releases for new British TV shows.

"How are you at making buttons?" my leader, Amy, asked me.

I had never made a button. Perhaps I was out of my element. I was already lacking in camp-counseling savvy. I also had no idea how to layer a s'more, make hemp bracelets, or sing the lyrics to "Cat's Cradle" at a fireside sing-along.

"It's easy," Amy said, demonstrating how to layer the button elements into the button press. "Every kid's going to make a button and you just put it together for them."

It looked and sounded easy enough, but by the third button I was already a colossal failure in the world of button-crafting.

"What happened?" one girl said, looking at her freshly pressed button. Her delicate splashes of glitter paint had flattened in the press and smeared across the surface of the button, covering the design she had so carefully drawn.

"Oh no," I said. "Do you want to make another one?"

The next button didn't adhere correctly, leaving the two pieces of plastic with gaping holes.

"Oh my," I said. "You might have to make a third."

Two buttons were already ruined. I started putting every ounce of my being into pressing the buttons, and as my body is composed of a lot of ounces, we're talking a lot of manpower.

"Great button, Roy," I said to a boy after checking out his name on the paper. "That's a cool football."

"It's a dog," he said.

I was off to a great start.

I was relieved when it was announced that button time had ended and I went off to meet my group of four. This was the group I would be responsible for all week and it contained two five-year-old twin girls, Erin and Caitlin. The other two girls in our group, Marnie and Sally, were both six years old. We were alerted in advance that Marnie had leukemia, but I still wasn't prepared to encounter someone so young that she didn't even know the terminology with which to describe her affliction. We were making puppets that morning in preparation for a puppeteer company that was coming to put on a play for us in the afternoon. The morning was two hours of glitter explosions, felt mishaps, and questions like "what happens if you get glue in your eyelashes?"

By lunch I was wiped out and the kids were starved. Erin only wanted to eat croutons, Sally requested crouton-less salad, and three different kids spilled the juice from their fruit cups onto their pants. Then they all abandoned their food for a raucous game of hide-and-seek. Miraculously they all settled down when the puppets arrived. The puppet show was tailor-made for the crowd and dealt with two schoolkids who had cancer. Looking over the crowd, I could see that they were captivated, and some even went up at the end to high-five the puppets. When their parents came to pick them up, the kids showed off the puppets they had made and dragged me over to meet their parents. "See you tomorrow," I said, hoping I'd have the energy for another round.

The next day we headed to a spring fair. When I was younger, every summer my parents would buy discounted tickets from their workplaces, pack my siblings and me up in the car with juice boxes, and take us for a day at a nearby amusement park. We always complained that we didn't have time to do enough when there, not noticing that my parents rarely went on the rides themselves, following us from one to the other and holding our visors and jackets as we stood in hour-long lines. That would be my role today.

When we got to the fair, we surveyed the carnival games, rides, and row upon row of candy vendors. We were going to have a great time, if only we could decide where to begin.

Every kid wanted to go on a different ride. If Erin wanted to go on the monkey scrambler, her twin, Caitlin, vetoed it. Marnie and Sally wanted to go on the scarier rides, which led to tears for little Sally. At six, she had the guts for it but unfortunately not the height. Finally we all settled upon the giant slide, which required you to slide down in optimal comfort and style in a burlap sack. "Come with us!" the twins said to me. I wasn't particularly interested in a ride made just for kids, but as Amy had told us in training, "Think about what the kids want." The kids wanted me on that slide. So I sat down on the center of the three slides, grabbed my burlap, and said, "Here we go!" As the little girls raced down their respective slides, their giggles of delight followed them over the bumps. I pushed off, expecting a leisurely ride down, but was immediately alarmed at how much speed I was picking up. As I went over the first bump, I lifted off the slide an inch and landed with a thud, continuing at breakneck speed. Conscious of the campers waiting for me at the bottom, I plastered a fake smile on my face that was masking my sheer terror.

When I hit the bottom, my burlap death trap kept sliding so far that I had to put my feet up to break my momentum at the fence.

"Wasn't that great?" Caitlin said, grabbing my hand. I was too shocked to respond.

That was the first of three slides I went down at the fair. I also went into fun houses and held shoes while various jumpy castles were tested. Although we were there for only five hours, I felt as if I had been born in the spring fair, attended school there, been married and divorced twice, and climbed Mount Kilimanjaro within its precincts. The kids, however, were as energized as when we arrived, and turbo-shocked by a treat of cotton candy at the end of the day. If this was the energy level we would hit every day, I wasn't sure I would make it through the week.

Marnie closed her eyes on the streetcar ride back and I worried that a full day of walking had tired her out. "Are you okay, Marnie?" I asked, kneeling by her seat.

"That was the best day ever," she replied. And with that one remark, all of my energy returned.

By midway through the week, I was in the swing of things. And I was so grateful that this was what my camp experience had ended up being. Not only was I getting to spend time with an amazing group of kids, I was getting to participate in a lot of the activities I had wanted to do when I was a kid.

On Thursday we were going to Medieval Times. This was a first for most of the kids, and for me as well. There had been only one opportunity to visit Medieval Times when I was in school—it was scheduled as an alternative to the senior prom. The guys who chose to go considered it a no-brainer. Watching jousting was a better use of an evening than standing against a wall in an uncomfortable tuxedo. For girls, it was considered social suicide. You would likely be the only member of your sex there. And regardless of whether you were a geek in normal life, on that night you would be considered a loser for not bringing your own sword.

"Will you sit beside me at the show, Sally?" I asked her on our bus ride over. She had spent the whole week glued to her brother Matthew's side and I was hoping the show would make her feel more comfortable relating to the others.

"Can I sit with Matthew?" she said.

We had made ourselves flags to cheer on our knights, avoiding the costly souvenir flags that they sold at the venue. I pointed Sally to the seat beside mine, which she took, but she kept looking back to keep an eye out for her brother.

The lights started dimming and the kids knew the main attraction was about to begin. Sally and Marnie, on either side of me, started to wave their flags as the knights rode out into the dirt arena. In perfect dinner-theater timing, the garlic bread also arrived at this same moment. The horses pranced around while the knights hammed it up for cheers from their sections. When the Red Knight stood in front of our section and raised his arms like a victorious gladiator, the kids screamed and clapped.

A tiny finger poked my left arm. "Is it done now?" Sally said, concerned that the show was over.

"Oh no," I said. "There's so much more. Don't worry, it just started."

"Okay," she said, smiling.

Little did Sally know how much was left in the show. As

we ripped our food apart with our hands, the knights all fought wildly choreographed fight scenes, straight out of a Dark Ages WWE match. Punches would send them flying across the arena. A sword that grazed them lightly sent them to their deaths. And all the while the kids cheered the Red Knight and booed his opponents.

"Is it done?" Sally said after the Yellow Knight fell to the ground.

"Nope," I said, "There's still more."

"Okay, thanks," she said, focusing back on the arena.

Before the final battle, the show took a pause for the king's servant to give shout-outs to various members of the audience.

"Lady Stephanie and Lady Mona are both turning seven today," he said. "And Lord Vijay is nine. Happy Birthday with love from Mummy, Daddy, and . . . Bibi . . . ji." His pronunciation was horrifying, but as there wouldn't have been any Indian knights in medieval times anyway, it was forgiven. "Lady Catherine is thirty today," he said as a group of drunken adults jumped up to point out the birthday girl. I wondered why Lady Catherine and her friends weren't at work, as we were at the 2 P.M. show, but the fact that two of her friends were play-fighting with swords behind her made me realize they might march to the beat of a different social norms drum.

"The Crescent Hill Day School's here today," the announcer continued, "as well as the Bay Ridge Day Camp."

"Will he say Gilda's?" the kids asked me. "I hope he says Gilda's."

Hoping for their chance to be recognized, the kids listened intently as he rattled off names. They wanted to cheer. They wanted and deserved the chance to cheer and be cheered by the rest of the auditorium.

"St. Anthony's Camp's here," the announcer said as I grew anxious.

The announcer continued to rattle off the list of school and camp groups and I could feel myself tensing up with each subsequent name, fearful that the list was ending. Were we supposed to have told them it was a special trip at the door? I wondered. Was there a way I could tell them now? All of the other kids in the stadium were standing proudly as their respective group names were called.

"What about Gilda's?" Marnie said to me.

Yes, what about Gilda's? I thought, looking up at the podium. Please say it, please, please say it. Let them have their chance to be cheered.

"I don't know," I said, clutching the extra flags I had made.

"Will they say it?" she asked.

"I hope so," I said.

"Our Lady of Lourdes Day Camp is here," the announcer said, "and Gilda's Club!"

The kids jumped out of their seats and waved their flags for everyone to see. "Wooo!" they cheered. "Wooooooo, Gilda's!"

Then, to top it off, the Red Knight won the tournament.

The kids were brimming with excitement on our way out. Like every other kid waiting in the foyer, they started fighting each other with their flags.

"Take that!"

"I'm the Red Knight!"

It was easy to forget that they weren't exactly like every

other kid in the arena that day. They had the same love of candy and joy for life, but they had one thing that separated them from others, a weight on their tiny shoulders. For the most part, we didn't talk about the C-word at camp. The children had weekly meetings where they talked about their feelings, and this was their week just to have fun. But if they wanted to talk about it, we did.

"Why did you come to Gilda's?" a girl named Lillian asked me on our bus ride home.

"Camp sounded like fun," I said. "I wanted to come be a part of it."

"No," she said. "Why did you come to *Gilda's*?"

"Oh," I said, finally understanding. "My grandmother had cancer. And two of my friends."

"Oh," she said. "Are they okay now?"

"Not my grandmother," I said. "But she was grandma age," I added. "But my friends are both great. They've been fine for a long time now."

"That's good," Lillian said, smiling.

My grandmother was actually only in her early sixties when we found out she had a brain tumor. The week before she had been moving sofas in the basement of my uncle's house and slipping us money to order pizza when our parents wouldn't allow us to get any. She was fit, still adept at transcribing our soaps for us, and only recently started wearing eyeglasses, as well as the dentures that we would find sitting on tables sometimes because she didn't like the way they felt in her mouth.

A fall took her to the doctor's office, where the diagnosis was given. They told us plainly that she would die, and soon.

She went for surgery to slow it down, but it was going to attack again.

I was in my first year of college and went home to see her one weekend in October. "You aren't going to come back," she told me as I said good-bye to her at the end of it. "You won't come back." She was implying, like all Indian grandmothers do, that I didn't visit often enough. But that would be the last time I would ever see her.

My dad, tasked with the responsibility of decision as the eldest child, boarded a plane to India with her so she could see my uncle and my grandfather, from whom she had lived apart for nearly two decades. My grandfather had tried to adapt to Canada but never took to it, so opted to stay in India. My grandmother adjusted more easily to her adopted home.

We had joked over the years that Bibi had become Westernized. She never adopted Western dress, but she would only drink Canada Dry Ginger Ale. If you gave her any other brand, she would push the glass away and say that it tasted like *pashab* (urine). She developed a fondness for gummy candies that were shaped and flavored like oranges and lemons and dotted with sugar, and we would force her to watch *Benny Hill*, just to entertain ourselves at her disgust when Benny chased nurses around fields. She would always laugh, knowing we were setting her up. She actually spent almost as much of her adult life in Canada as she did in India, but in her heart, India was her home. She was born there, and two months after I last saw her, she died there.

My dad was devastated by her death. He, and all his siblings, only ever spoke about her with extreme love and reverence. Despite their stories of being chased around the farm by her as she wielded a stick to hit them, they had all been very close to her. My siblings and I were actually closer to her than we were to our own parents, so it was a pretty big blow for everyone.

The kids at Gilda's had such a less emotional view of cancer than most adults do. For them, it just existed. It was what it was. When I grabbed Marnie's hand, she would sometimes say that I had taken her "sick hand," a hand weakened by her many treatments. That was her explanation; she was simply sick. It was a part of her life, as was school, friends, and loving *Hannah Montana*.

The next day was our last and we shepherded the campers to the north of the city to watch Robert Munsch plays performed. We found spots on the floor.

"I can't see," Erin said, jumping into my lap.

"Okay," I said. "Now let's be quiet. It's starting."

I think the play was good, but I could barely watch because my legs were falling asleep. I spent most of the time kneading my thighs to ward off the pins and needles.

"Let's get up and dance," the actors said.

"Dance time," I said, pushing Erin off my lap. I did the Hokey Pokey with extreme force to try to revive my legs and found Erin a nice seat in front of me for the rest of the play.

In the afternoon, we all worked together to make a mural on which we inscribed the Gilda's Club slogan: "Cancer Sucks." The kids painted, cut and pasted, and wrote their feelings about cancer all over the canvas, which was later hung up to commemorate our days at the camp.

At the end of the day, the parents gathered outside to pick up their kids, who were all saying bye to one another. Some of the kids would see each other again in the Tuesday-night group, but they didn't all attend.

"Bye!" I said to the twins as they hugged their mom's legs.

"Thanks for all the fun at Medieval Times," I said to Sally as she walked to her car.

"Bye," she said, waving.

"Marnie," I said, "your mom's here."

Marnie and her pigtailed little sister walked to the car.

"Good-bye and thank you," Marnie said. "I hope I see you again in my life."

It was I who owed them the thanks. I had a week of fun and laughs. I got to try new things and meet new people and feel like a part of something special. Camp completely exceeded my expectations, which says a lot, considering that they had been building for almost twenty years.

→ TWELVE ←

gimme a break!

One thing I was learning about goals was that most people think of them the way they think about abstract notions. They are New Year's resolutions and weight-loss pledges on sticky notes that peel off the fridge long after the goal has already been abandoned. As long as you don't attempt to reach a goal, it's always there hovering in the distance. But I wish I had known so many years ago what it felt like not only to move toward a goal but to actually cross the finish line. It felt amazing. It made the next goal seem attainable and the larger one after that suddenly seem like it was doable. It made huge life dreams seem like just another set of goals that you could actually go out and attain. This realization was having a very profound effect on me.

It had been only six months but so much can change in six

months. Since my birthday, I had been thinking about what I wanted from life, a conversation I had with myself after every birthday. I didn't know what I wanted but I knew I wanted something more than I currently had. I liked my job, but I always felt like I was a background player supporting people who were making the product that I loved.

My workplace had begun an unpaid leave-of-absence program, partially due to the company's financial state. This offered a great opportunity for me to do some real soul-searching.

My greatest worry was that I would waste the feeling of achievement and satisfaction that I now felt. Each new thing I learned, each skill I crossed off my list of goals, left me energized and anticipating the next challenge. I didn't want to get to the end of that road and feel like I was back at the same dead end. This had to be part of a bigger picture.

Work had made up too much of my identity for too long. It ate up my week, it woke me up in the middle of the night, and it demanded so much of me, though it was no longer giving me the equivalent in pleasure or fulfillment. Lately, though, I had begun to look at work differently. It was the nine hours before I could dance, the two weeks before I could go to camp. I had moved from living to work to working to live. Although so much had changed for me personally in the past six months, professionally everything droned on as it had the year before and as it would the year after. This was becoming harder for me to accept. Maybe I needed to shake up my life in a bigger way. I could travel, think, and be sure of what I wanted to do, instead of just keeping on doing what I was doing, for no reason but inertia. I had savings enough to last me a few months, and time off would let me take a much-needed pause and digest the past six months, and consider what lay ahead for me in the next few years.

After mulling it over for weeks, I decided I would ask for a leave, but I was wary of how my request would play out. It was still up to the department head to allow leaves, and hearing that a publicist who covered a fourth of their channels would be missing for three months would not exactly thrill them. But, I reasoned, I deserved this break. I had worked hard and diligently for nearly five years. I was a dedicated and trusted member of the team and I was hopeful that my superiors would be understanding. I looked online at my department head's calendar for a meeting time. There was hardly one blank space on it for the next two weeks, but I managed to squeeze myself into a slot on a Thursday afternoon.

I had a few days to try to compose my thoughts, but just couldn't put them perfectly into words. How do you explain to someone that you simply felt different from the person you used to be? When I started out the year, I had expected to have a few new skills and a few funny stories to share at dinner parties. But I was surprised not only by how much my recent experiences were changing me, but by how important they were becoming to me.

When Thursday rolled around, I was cool as a cucumber. Sitting in my boss's office, I readied myself for a discussion about how best to handle things in the office during my months off. I had notes on a few ideas of my own, ideas I thought would impact the department in the most beneficial way and offer new opportunities to those who were seeking them.

"What's up?" she asked.

I took this as my cue and went into a spiel so moving it could have been a deleted scene from *Steel Magnolias*. From childhood dreams of an immigrant's daughter to realizations reached while wandering in a lush green village in India, I wove a story so beautiful I could already picture Kate Winslet in the lead role of the movie version. The delivery may have been a tad syrupy and thick, but the core of it was sincere. In short, I told her, I really needed to take a leave. I was at a crossroads after embarking on what I thought would be a handful of fun activities, but had now become a journey that was taking me places I had never imagined.

"I've thought this through so many times," I said, finally getting to the heart of the matter. "If I could have three months off, I'd be so grateful. I know it's a lot to ask, but I've been dedicated to this place since the moment I started and I would return even more dedicated."

I took a breath. I had said my piece. I really hoped that she would agree because if I couldn't get the time off, I might not actually be able to finish all of my goals. I had no vacation time left and still had to do some of the larger activities on my list. I didn't want to abandon my list of goals and return to my humdrum working-stiff existence without at least one more goal under my belt. This had to be different.

I don't recall exactly what my boss said, just that it was not what I wanted to hear. She couldn't go along with my proposal. Three months was simply too long. I could be spared for a month at the most, preferably December, which was still five months away. She asked me to figure out how I could make it work and let her know.

"What're you going to do now?" Jen and Jaclyn asked me at lunch.

"I haven't the slightest clue," I said. "I really don't see how I could do this all in one month. I have to tell her how I'm going to make this leave of absence work as soon as I can, but I just have no idea."

That weekend, I holed up in my apartment with all of my thinking tools: a mountain of junk food to stimulate my brain and a pile of classic seventies horror films for when I needed a break. I was big on thinking important decisions through with the thoroughness of a police detective trying to crack a big case. My living room looked like the conference room at a business convention with charts and pie graphs and to-do lists scattered and posted in every nook and cranny.

I was so incredibly confused. The company had created this leave-of-absence program, which I was aware that people in other departments had taken advantage of. One girl in another department had been given four months off to go backpacking in Australia. How was that more valid than my request? I guess I had overestimated my importance at the company. It was naive to think that a large corporation had the same regard for me that I held for it for the past five years. A company's purpose is to make money, not worry about the life plans of its employees. My superiors were looking out for themselves. I had to look out for myself and for my future, which was a difficult task, as I had no idea what I wanted from it.

I was at an impasse. I needed some counsel.

Unfortunately, most people I spoke to advised me to do the same thing: quit. This was not on my list of preferred options. It was a leap way too large to contemplate. Yet the more I thought about it, the more I felt there was no other viable option.

"Just quit," one sister advised.

"Definitely don't quit," another countered.

I was beyond confused. "Would *you* do it?" I would ask those who suggested I leave. After silence, then contemplation, the answer became much grayer for them. Advice is often very black and white until you have to imagine the scenario as being your own. I wanted to stay with the company. I needed to work. But I wanted this leave time more.

I wanted a chance to slice something extraordinary out of my increasingly ordinary life, but I wasn't willing to alter the trajectory of my career to get it. I was an ordinary person. I woke up at seven-thirty, wiped the sleep from my eyes, and went to work. I had three weeks of the year that were my own; the rest belonged to whoever signed my check. This was the only life I knew, and although it was routine and at times stifling, it was what was comfortable.

But what if I was meant for something different from this? If I wasn't, it was okay, I was happy enough with my life, but I could no longer be happy to not try. I met Jaclyn and Maggie because we had all studied TV writing and production together. We had dreams of being creative, but then after a year of dead-end jobs, I was so happy to get my foot in the door at my present job that I settled into a backseat role, writing and producing press materials to celebrate other people's creativity. Who knows, maybe during those three months I could finally try to delve into it myself? Maybe it wouldn't be for me, but I wanted to try. Swimming and dancing and catching up with the other kids were my yearlong goals. This was my lifelong goal.

I was raised to be realistic. Indian women aren't dreamers. They are encouraged to pursue three lines of work: medicine, accounting, or baby making. Anything else is considered a waste of time. Pursuing a move to real television production wasn't realistic, but the fact that I'd even get around to pursuing it was also unrealistic. Even I thought it was a bit of a dreamer's dream, but who knew what I was supposed to be doing in life? If the last six months had taught me anything, it was that I was the only one who could make my life what I wanted it to be, and I was the one who would live with the consequences of it not being fulfilling.

But—and there's always a *but*—I liked my job and had struggled to get there. With so many people out of work, I was more than grateful to have a job at all. Businessmen were working part-time as janitors, ex-accountants were making deliveries. It wasn't the time to take risks. I still had to pay off my student loan. I wanted to put more money into my retirement account. I hadn't been on a proper, relaxing vacation for years. Walking away meant the end of financial security, which at my salary was still more of a monetary aspiration than a reality.

On Monday morning, I walked into my boss's office and said the two words I had been agonizing over for the past week: "I quit." As they came out of my mouth, it was as if I was having an out-of-body experience. I couldn't believe it but it was done. I offered over a month's notice. I would stay until the end of August and then I would be cast out into the world, jobless, clueless, and full of hope and excitement. I was ready. In fact, I couldn't wait.

→ THIRTEEN ←

(leaving) the office

For the next week I felt like hurling myself at my boss's feet to beg for mercy, but I stuck to my guns. I had been cautious and practical my whole life and it was time to take the opposite approach. Don't underestimate how much you change once you achieve a goal. With every swing of the racquet, every tap step, and every minute behind the wheel, I was becoming more confident and ready to tackle the next step.

Sure, my goals were not as grand as trying to climb a mountain, but that is what made the victory that much sweeter to me. These were things I had simply ruled out as experiences that I had simply missed, with no chance of recovery. I had defined myself as that person who couldn't swim and had never been to Disney World, but now I was beginning to understand that I could still create those memories and redefine myself. It was a snowball effect of my newfound confidence that gave me the sheer audacity to walk away from my job into total uncertainty.

I told my parents that I had taken a leave of absence because Indians cannot leave paying work unless they have been dead at least a week and even that can be considered a flimsy excuse. I knew I was doing the best thing for myself, but thirty years of experience told me that my parents weren't the type of people who would chuck responsibility for adventure and personal growth. Had they been students in Robin Williams's class in *Dead Poets Society,* the second the kids jumped up onto their desks to "Seize the Day!" my parents would have sprinted out of the room to get the headmaster.

Also, old habits die hard and I guess a part of me still felt a bit guilty admitting that I had thrown away stability and responsibility to indulge a whim. This had never been an option in my parents' lives. No doubt my father would have loved to continue the classes he took at the University of Toronto and become a professor in Canada, as he had been planning to do in India. But he had to work to make money for his family, so it wasn't an option. My mother and father never went on vacations, they didn't have expensive cars or jewelry, and I could count on one hand the number of times they had ever eaten in a restaurant in their lives. One meal with my father drinking gravy like soup would substantiate this claim for any nonbelievers.

On their meager salaries, they saved to have enough money to help their children out with their college expenses. And here I was spitting on their very belief system by putting a fantasy before reality and responsibility. But in the end, I knew it was the right thing to do, for myself. My parents would have to make peace with my decision.

Taking a leap of faith had a wonderful effect on me. The month of August felt as if the earth had been reprogrammed especially for my enjoyment. The sun shone brighter. The birds chirped more melodically and the breeze always smelled like lilacs and lilies.

I was enthused. It was the shake-up my tired life sorely needed.

"What will you do?" people asked me.

"You know, I'm not sure yet." I would smile. "But I have some ideas."

In actuality, I had one incredibly crazy idea. An idea so far-fetched that I tried to push it out of my mind. It was preposterous, juvenile, and likely shared by every teenager who has ever seen a local production of *Rent*.

I wanted to move to New York. I'd wanted to move to the city since I had traveled there for my senior-class high school trip. I had saved up for that trip for months, working in the high-stakes world of cashiering at Walmart to ensure I had the proper spending money for all the black-and-white cookies my heart desired. We drove down on a giant school bus, a twelve-hour ride that breezed by because of the promise of what lay at the end. The second we exited onto the bustling Manhattan street, I was in love. Deeply, madly in love. It was March, a month normally dreary, but the lights twinkling in front of the department stores and the distinct luminescence of the snow were so magically New York that it felt like living in a snow globe.

I was eighteen, from a small city in Canada, and wearing

that country's uniform of large ski jacket, oversize corduroy pants, and a sweatshirt. And yet I felt as glamorous as the women wearing Burberry tweed and walking their poodles on the Upper West side. I oohed and aahed at the majestic twin towers. I asked poignant political questions during the UN tour. I snapped photos of the beautiful tree in front of Rockefeller Center and got lost in the beauty of the majestic snow-covered trees in the park.

On our first evening there, we were all standing beside our bus waiting to travel down to a Broadway show. A comedian from a nearby comedy club saw a captive audience and walked over to entice us to come to his show. After entertaining us with a few prepackaged G-rated jokes, he turned his attention to me.

Studying my a-little-bit-too-light skin and science-experiment-gone-wrong-colored eyes, he looked at me and said, "You're half something and half something."

Wanting to clear up that I was in fact 100 percent Indian, I replied, "No, I'm all something."

"I can seeeeee thatttttt," he drawled in a flirty tone that made me blush despite the fact that he was brazenly homosexual and no doubt recycling a bit he had used on ethnic audience members a hundred times.

But back then, in my mind, this was classic New York: there were hilarious interactions at every turn, with friendly banter straight out of a sitcom. The mayor would high-five you on the street corners and strangers would link arms and croon show tunes as they rode the subway together.

My vision of New York hadn't changed since that first visit and I desperately wanted to return. I wanted to feel that same schoolgirl delight and sense of possibility. But it felt as outlandish as Quasimodo coming down from the bell tower and saying, "I'm leaving now, to pursue my modeling career in Paris."

But then, was it really that ridiculous? My whole year thus far was bordering on the absurd and now I had gone so far as to quit my job to continue pursuing a path that was getting less and less marked. If that wasn't insane, I didn't know what was. Moving to New York would be the insane icing on top of my quarter-life crisis cake and yet I found myself seriously considering it.

→ FOURTEEN ←

the wonder (what i was thinking) years

I had actually made one very ill-planned attempt to move to New York a decade earlier. All throughout my adolescence, I had been a drama nerd. In the fifth grade, I walked home three kilometers, three nights a week, in the stark dark winter nights, all to be in the chorus of our school production of *Snow White and the Seven Dwarfs.* In high school, I was involved in anything and everything, because my alternative was sitting at home watching the same reruns I'd already seen ten times each. Once my parents understood that a student needed to be well rounded to get into a good college, they gave up on trying to keep us at home. We still weren't allowed to go out socially, but I volunteered twice a week, I worked at a doughnut store on the weekends, and at school I belonged to the poster-making club, the student council, the intramural sports committee, and any other club that would take me.

But the bulk of my extracurricular time went to drama. I was in the school plays, the drama festivals, school assemblies, and any classroom demonstration that might have required my thespian touch. When I graduated high school I was given an award for my dramatic contributions. I even quoted *Seinfeld* in my valedictory address. Looking back at my old high school yearbook last month, I had totally forgotten the two categories I had won in the all-knowing "most likely to" section. I would have guessed "most likely to grow a handlebar mustache" and "most likely to marry a cousin" myself.

But there I was, listed as both "most likely to become a stand-up comedian" and "most likely to have their own TV show." This, of course, meant I was destined for success. Although it's more than likely that at least half of past winners in similar "most likely to" categories at their respective schools are living in their parents' basements, I have to look at myself as the exception, not the rule.

But to me, writing and doing plays was just clowning around, and college, with all of its competitiveness and costs, was a time to get serious. I chose my major of international relations and headed off to the groves of academe to figure out what the hell that actually meant. I had a great time in college and met some of my closest lifelong friends there. But college was also when I completely lost my focus.

I was so busy trying to keep my head above water in a sea of students so much smarter and harder working than I was. I joined a few extracurricular clubs, particularly those that would allow me to write, but for the most part, I became entwined in the collegiate activities of navel-gazing, oversleeping, and trying to map out a future.

In the end, I graduated more lost than when I began, and returned home to fulfill a cliché of my generation and live in my parents' basement. While others went off to graduate school or trekked across Europe, I spent months waking up at eleven, avoiding people who might possibly ask me what I was doing, and sending out as many résumés as my dot-matrix printer could sputter out.

One day, after two months of barely emerging from my basement room, I heard a knock on the door. I was working on applying for yet another job, hijacking the phone line to access the dial-up Internet, when my dad popped his head in.

"You know," he said, "you can go do things. You don't have to always sit around here. I can take you places if you need to go."

Sure, I wanted to say, having wished I had been told this eight years ago. *Why don't we go to the new martini bar downtown and get some cosmopolitans?*

"I'm okay," I said as I reread a cover letter. "I need to keep looking for a job."

It was obvious that my dad, who was usually the last family member to pick up on emotional cues, thought I was depressed. And I no doubt was. University didn't let me be the shining student I had been up to that point, but it kept me busy and on a track to something. Upon graduating, I was hit with the realization that I could no longer trace the track's route. This, coupled with being broke and being back at home, created the perfect recipe for Depression Pie. Which

I must have eaten a lot of, as I also gained nearly fifteen pounds that year, numbing my boredom with bags of chips and chocolate-covered anything.

Every month or so, Melodie would pick me up and we would go out to a local chain restaurant and talk about life and dreams over spinach dips and large margaritas.

"So what's new?" she would ask.

After sighing deeply, I would detail my previous two weeks.

"I've applied for another fifteen jobs," I said. "Never heard back from any of them."

"Are you working on any writing?" she asked.

Since we had both moved back to our respective homes, we decided we would pursue our creative desires in order to have something positive to show for our time there. Looking through my bookshelf one day, I found the birthday gift that Melodie had given me that year. It was a writing journal with the inscription "Remember me when you hit it big!" At that point I just wanted to hit anywhere but rock bottom, which was slowly inching closer.

"Have you seen anyone else lately?" she asked. My answer was always the same.

Other than Melodie, I had very little human contact with the outside world, so I just listened to her stories of the people we knew.

"Thanks for driving," I would say when she dropped me off, knowing the situation would never be reversed.

"No problem. Let's do it again soon."

After I'd been home for almost six months, penniless and now hopeless, my luck finally changed. I got a job interview at a local insurance company, and right before Christmas, I was told I had the job. That was the greatest Christmas present I could have hoped for—finally, I had a reason to wake up in the morning, an answer to the question of what I was doing, and a chance to make some much-needed cash.

I graduated college with a credit-card debt that kept me up nights, and after months of my hiding it, my parents figured it out via an "accidental" opening of my mail. I would have reported them for this federal offense except that after they lectured me endlessly, they kindly offered to pay the bill. The many-thousand-dollar bill.

Having never amassed consumer debt in their lives, they were horrified at the thought of my having to pay interest for two years, so I gratefully accepted their offer.

The only time I can recall my dad ever telling me he was proud of me was when, after several months at my new job, I handed him a check to clear my debt to him.

"That's great, kid," he said in English, to ensure that I understood his happiness. "That's great."

He expressed his pleasure at my responsibility, put the check in his closet, and hasn't cashed it to this day. It was a kind gesture, but I sincerely hope that the time that has passed has also rendered the check void because if my dad tried to cash it now, it would bounce higher than Pam Anderson running on the beach in a *Baywatch* montage.

Now gainfully employed, I would take two buses to work, rotating a small collection of manly button-down shirts with an even smaller collection of polyester pants. I knew I wasn't the picture of fashion, but after a fifty-year-old woman I worked with came up to me, pointed to her oxford shirt and ill-fitting black pants, and said, "Look, I'm wearing a Rupinder outfit," I really had to pause and take stock of my life.

I was in a job that was not for me, wearing the business-casual equivalent of mustard-stained jogging pants. I woke up each morning fifteen minutes before my bus left, slipped on my glasses, adjusted my bun, and grabbed my sandwich. I looked and felt forty years old.

I ate lunch alone, often going for a walk and listening to my Walkman. My coworkers were easily the nicest I have ever worked with, but I never socialized with them outside of work. While other twentysomethings would make plans with their friends for postwork drinks, my phone would ring every afternoon to offer a different proposition. At about 4 P.M., I would look down to see a familiar number pop up on my call display. It would be Sumeet, then ten years old, calling to tell me of the local fast-food specials of the evening.

"Okay," he would say, cutting out any type of salutation. "There is a two-for-one pizza special but there's also a meal deal for McDonald's."

I would laugh at this daily ritual but occasionally I caved and agreed to treat him to a grease fest. He would wait for my bus at a stop a few blocks from our house and we would walk over together to the mall to rot our stomachs with some form of fast food. Even after we consumed thousands of artery-clogging calories, the phone would ring again the next day like clockwork. I had to give my brother points for persistence.

After nine months of the job, I knew I was wasting the company's time. I didn't know what I would do next, but I knew that this wasn't for me. My parents weren't enthused when I told them I was going to quit in order to travel across

Asia with my high school chums Vern and Jessie. But at this point I was twenty-three years old, so my parents knew that they didn't have much say in the decision. I had saved enough money from my job to survive for my three-month trip and at least six months after, so I decided to do something daring and act my age again. I worried that my lack of enthusiasm would result in my getting fired from that job in the end, so I knew that I had to preserve whatever self-esteem I had by getting out on my own terms.

This is when I first got the idea in my head to actually make the move to New York. As I walked down Khaosan Road in Bangkok, I imagined myself walking down Fifth Avenue instead, on my way to a great job, then later to meet friends for a great dinner. I didn't know what the hell I planned to do in Manhattan, but I knew I didn't want to work in insurance. I wanted to be artistic, and this would require the inspiration of hanging with beatnik poets and Broadway dancers, singing show tunes until the wee hours.

Of course, things don't always work out as planned, and when I got home, I waited a week, then decided to hit my parents with the news. I knew full well that they thought of New York as a cesspool of crime and depravity based on nothing but their imaginations and a *Dateline* special or two. Because of this, I knew that I had to soften the blow, and when it comes to blow softening, there's no better cushion than a parent-friendly white lie.

"I got a job offer!" I told my parents as they were sitting and watching an Indian program on TV one night.

Seeing smiles on their faces, I saw my window of opportunity. "It's in New York."

"It is?" they asked, awaiting the explanation of this mystery job that had found me just a week after I returned from my trip to Asia.

"Yes," I said, lying through my teeth. "It's in marketing. It's a great job."

They looked thoroughly unconvinced as they continued to drink their chai.

Before they could ask me any further questions about my new fictitious employer or my new fictitious job duties, I headed to my basement lair to work out some fictitious details.

I hadn't yet set a departure date, which was handy, as my plans were soon derailed by the power of parent-induced guilt. Two days later, my dad caught me as I was making myself a sandwich.

"I didn't sleep last night," he told me. He didn't want me to go to New York. To him, New York was scary.

"Fine!" I said through clenched teeth. "I'll tell them I'm not coming."

Because of my parents' neuroses, I had abandoned a great opportunity. It didn't matter that the job hadn't been real. It had been real to them, and though I might sit in the basement another six months, unemployed and unhappy, to them this was a lesser evil than living in a big city that they believed to be run by Mayor Beelzebub. I could have argued. I could have extolled the virtues of my new amazing fake job, but I knew it wasn't worth it. I had lost this battle. Parents always guilt kids with the sacrifices that they made for them. But kids are forced to make sacrifices too sometimes, to help make their parents' lives easier.

→ FIFTEEN ←

manhattan

This time, nothing was going to stop me from getting there. "I'm thinking of coming to New York," I told Madeleine, who had recently relocated to the Big Apple.

"Do it!" she said.

"Okay, you've convinced me," I said. "Now find me an apartment. And make it cheap." My savings would only stretch so far, but I could comfortably do two months there. She laughed, so I didn't tell her that I was serious, and she soon found herself checking out apartments for me like my part-time Realtor.

I decided to waste no time and finish work on a Friday, then move to New York on the following Monday. Jaclyn's wedding was a few days before my departure, so I would stay for that, then jump on a plane for my own solo honeymoon.

The bird-chirping bright-skyed August soon gave way to frantic weeks of trying to wrap up my job and plan a move to another city. My phone was ringing off the hook, I had committed to finishing two major press announcements, and I was helping a colleague create fall plans to launch several big-budget shows on the networks we covered. I was still researching camps and Disney vacations in my evening hours but now had added the task of trolling Internet sites for New York City sublets below a million dollars a month. After doing this unsuccessfully for a number of weeks, I started to think that maybe a million for a studio apartment in Queens was fair, as long as the utilities were included.

My friend Melissa, who had taken the TV writing program with me, had moved to New York after getting married. She sent out e-mails to all of her NYC friends to ask if they knew of any good places to rent. It was obvious that it was going to take a village to make this happen. In the meantime, I was working ten hours a day to ensure that all of my work was finished, and coming in on weekends to start the daunting process of cleaning out my desk. One drawer was filled with candy. Another contained a pharmacy worth of lotions and potions, while the floor under my desk was covered with pairs of shoes. As I pulled off my nameplate and shoved my shoes in a box, it hit me that there was really no way to turn back now.

The last two weeks of August were a testament to effective time management, a skill that I will now list on my résumé twice, as I believe myself to be quite proficient at it. Work got wrapped up, plane tickets were purchased, plans were set, arrangements were made, and everything started to fall into place.

During this time, I sent Madeleine out to check out an apartment for me. She had moved to New York the year before and settled in the East Village. The apartment she looked at on my behalf was available until the end of October and was partially furnished, extremely reasonable, and in Williamsburg, the hipster capital of the universe. I wanted to live up by Central Park, but Melissa lived in Williamsburg and Madeleine was only two subway stops away, so it seemed an ideal alternate location. The pictures looked decent—it was a small space but recently renovated and the kitchen looked new.

"Are you sure you want to live in Williamsburg?" Madeleine asked me after seeing the place. She liked it but wondered if I would soon start wishing I were living near the big willow trees that lined the park.

"Oh, I'll get over it," I advised. "Just take it."

Five minutes later she called back again. "Are you sure?" she asked. "You've said for weeks that you want to live up by the park. Are you sure you aren't going to regret that?"

If I took a place by the park, it would be more expensive, and I would regret the extra cost. If I took the place in Williamsburg, I would likely wish I had lived by the park. I was already aware of this. "Just take it," I said. "I don't want to spend forever on this and I'm sure you don't want to look at ten more places for me."

And with that, I now had a roof over my head and my relocation to New York had turned from fantasy to reality. The next week I was duly honored at work with not just one farewell event, but four: there was the official work good-bye meeting, the official work good-bye party, the good-bye lunch, and the after-work good-bye karaoke. The official good-bye took place on the beautiful patio attached to one of the upper floors of our office building. In the scorching-hot sun, my coworkers and I stood in a circle while a cake melted behind us and held up plastic glasses of sparkling wine. My bosses and managers all praised me and said good-bye. I inadequately reciprocated, as there was no way I could summarily express my feelings.

"Thanks, everyone," I said, looking out at the crowd of people in front of me. "I really can't express enough how much I've loved working here. I've learned so much. I've met some amazing people here, some of whom are now among my closest friends. Every day I walked into this building, I walked out loving my job. Not many people can say that."

I paused when it finally hit me that I was giving my good-bye speech.

"I'll really miss all of you so much. This has been an amazing five years, and I wish you all so much success and happiness in life."

I hoisted my glass and they followed suit. I was closing the chapter on five years of my life and five years is a long time, as Josef Stalin knew. It was a bittersweet farewell, I thought, sipping my now hot white wine. And sigh, I would miss the free wine.

The after-work good-bye party is really where the action happens. The party during the day is a one-drink-and-back-to-the-desk affair. It's after work that people let loose. And on a scale of one to ten, this one registered a twelve. The fact that a minitornado was ripping through the city of Toronto and rendering it wisest to stay at the bar and not venture outside acted to ensure that the night contained all of the ludicrous, alcohol-fueled moments that are features of every decent work party. Bottles were ordered, shots were consumed, speech became slurred, confessions were shared, and the general merriment frequently crept past the fine line between endearing and inappropriate.

"I wish I could do what you're doing," one coworker after another said after a few too many beverages. We would clink glasses and express our mutual admiration before I headed to the next person to do the same. It was like a positive-affirmation square dance. After *far* too many beverages, some told me of their own plans to leave, or their desperate desire to do so.

This was not a shock to me. Every lottery commercial ever aired on television has the winner indulging in the same fantasy: leaving their job. Whether it's early retirement or a marching band announcing that they quit, the second their numbers are called, they get the hell out of cubicle Dodge. It is the *true* North American dream. As the trees were felled and power lines struck down, we all continued our lovefest, comforted by the barely depleted supply of alcohol surrounding us.

On my official last day on the job, I woke up earlier than normal with a weird sensation in my stomach. It was similar to the first-day-of-school butterflies I had experienced as a child, but this time the decisions involved had more serious consequences than deciding whether to wear the blue or orange turtleneck. I pulled on a dress and swept my mass of hair into a ponytail. Brushing some color onto my face to erase my lack of sleep, I spent a good minute staring at myself in the mirror. The woman looking back at me appeared the same as always, but inside I was completely new. Five years ago, I would have given anything for a full-time job that allowed me to sock a few dollars away into retirement funds and enjoy a dinner out with friends once a month. Now I was throwing everything I knew away and was unafraid of what that meant.

"Let's go," I yelled to Jen, who was waiting for me downstairs. I wanted this day to be done.

"This is our last time walking to work together," I said as we strolled our usual path to work. "This is the last croissant I'll get from this store on our walk to work," I noted as we entered my favorite bakery. I really loved those croissants. Although I was excited to embark on an adventure that would lead me in new directions, I knew I would miss the comfortable familiarity of my daily routine.

Luckily, I had done all that I needed to do ahead of schedule, out of sheer panic and a desire to make my absence less of a burden on others. This worked out well since my last day consisted of about two hours of official meetings, one hour for a lovely sushi meal with all of my fellow publicists, and three hours to clean out the dregs of personal items that were still left in my desk. For my good-bye tour, I bid farewell to as many people as I could. After my arms were exhausted from hugging, I packed up the last of my belongings, left my BlackBerry and access pass on my desk, and walked out of the office into the beautiful sunshine.

What the hell was I thinking? There was no turning back now. Security would tackle me if I tried to go back to work on Monday. Likely I would never see some of my coworkers again and I now was running the risk of being back where I was five years ago, working temp jobs and wondering if it would ever get better, but I had high hopes. This year was really opening my eyes to my own abilities. I was proud of myself for taking charge of my life and attempting to steer it back in the direction I desired. I wasn't just a dreamer; I was a person who was willing to work hard, who was aware she had a lot to learn, and who knew that people out there had exactly the lives they wanted. So why not me?

That night was the height of my weeklong good-bye extravaganza. A crew of my close work friends met for the ultimate in farewells: the karaoke. We sang until our throats were hoarse in a room that was private enough to make it appropriate to add coordinated dance moves.

I was going to miss this. Coworkers really make or break a job. We all took turns keeping a candy dish supplied and met for monthly sushi dates to get out of work once in a while. I would now have to eat lunch by myself, crack jokes to myself all day, tell myself to be quiet in meetings with myself, and gossip about myself to myself. I hated myself for still wondering if I had made a grave mistake.

The night ended with everyone singing Frank Sinatra's "New York, New York" as a farewell and good-luck gesture to me. We stood up, kicked our legs like chorus girls, and sashayed in a big finish. I was sure at this moment that I had made the right decision. Nobody ever sang about sitting in a cubicle.

part two

→ SIXTEEN ←

movin' on up to a deluxe apartment in the sky

Not wanting to waste any time, I boarded the plane for New York first thing Monday morning. I had just finished work on Friday, but when living a dream is involved, there's no time to spare. Having mapped out the area around my new apartment, all routes to it, and the nearest decent restaurants, I landed at the airport and did what I always did in a city to feel like a local: I took the subway. This would have been a breeze had it not been for the two giant suitcases I was lugging.

The apartment was a walk-up, like many in the city. Huffing and puffing my way up five flights, I walked into an apartment that was cute, but lacked the comforts of home. The bedroom contained a bed with no sheets on it, and the only other furniture was a sofa and coffee table.

There was not one picture on the wall or rug on the floor and the cupboards contained a skeleton crew of dishes. No TV, radio, or Internet assured that I would be both undistracted and unaware if Godzilla attacked the city. The place had all the warmth and coziness of a drug front, but I would make do for two months.

Madeleine had asked me several times if I was sure I wanted to live in Williamsburg, and in the end, my budget won out over my desire for leafy green beauty and ivy-covered town homes. Williamsburg offered me the maximum bang for my minuscule buck. But as I stood in my new apartment, I recalled why I'd wanted to live in Manhattan in the first place. I had never desired to live in hip Manhattan—SoHo, the Lower East Side, or the East Village. I wanted to live in the quiet, senior-citizen and family-filled upper Manhattan, where the nightlife was limited to restaurants and wine bars, the museums were all within walking distance, and in every direction there was the park. To me, Manhattan was all about the beautiful, glorious park, where families sat with picnic baskets, new love blossomed in the winding paths, and children pushed sailboats in the pond.

Williamsburg is incredible. It's where all the newest bars and coolest restaurants open. It's where everyone wants to be on Saturday nights and where old couch potatoes like me who like to go to sleep by eleven are just wasting real estate. In Williamsburg, graffiti-covered walls adorn the exteriors of the coolest concert venues, thrift shops, and bars. It has its share of adorable families and people of all ages, but it can definitely also claim more than its share of men with giant beards, walking with their arms draped around the shoulders of teeny-weeny girls with messy hair and thick-framed glasses, wearing tiny thrift-shop dresses. One person out-cooled the other and I looked like Steve Urkel from *Family Matters* in comparison.

I was more than fine with that, as I already knew I wasn't cool. I didn't desire to be cool. I hadn't the patience for making sure my bangs were just so, researching the latest and greatest bands, and wearing barely-there leggings as if they were real pants.

My first evening in New York consisted of sweeping, mopping, and trying to arrange bits of my clothing and books to give the apartment a lived-in feel. Later I met Melissa for some much-needed sushi at a local restaurant. As I didn't really know my way around Williamsburg, I wandered the deserted streets for a while to get my bearings. This is a major difference between Williamsburg and Manhattan. Whereas Manhattan is always a sea of people, parts of Williamsburg are so quiet you can hear the crickets being mugged by the cockroaches. There are one or two main drags that are always busy, but parts in between are perfect if you want absolute quiet or an ideal location for your new home in the Witness Protection Program. No matter, I told myself while walking to meet Mel. I was going to head into the city most days, as I had no intention of sitting around my abandoned apartment.

"Welcome to New York," Melissa exclaimed when she saw me. "We're happy to have you."

"I'm happy to finally be here!" I said.

After we stuffed ourselves with sushi, I returned home, threw my new bedding onto the bed, and dove into it. At least the bed was comfortable. I can deal with anything if the bed is comfortable.

In the middle of the night I got up to get a glass of water. I flipped on the kitchen light and opened the fridge. Beside my water jug was a cockroach.

"Oh God, oh God, oh God," I said as I slammed the door shut. I was aware that roaches were common in New York, but in the *fridge*? That was just too much.

The fridge was my sacred place. How could I ever buy an on-sale birthday cake again and joyfully lick its icing and eat a slice each night alone? Now a roach would be sitting on its plastic casing, assuming that it too would receive a piece. I knew that New York had lenient rules for squatters, but no way in hell were these roaches going to stay.

"Get out!" I screamed, opening the door and swatting at it. It scurried in circles on the fridge shelf but did not retreat. I finally steeled myself, seized a wad of paper towels, and grabbed the roach. Depositing it in the garbage, I went back to the fridge, used paper towels to hold the water jug, and poured a glass. I stumbled back to bed, resetting my alarm for an hour earlier so I could clean out the whole fridge.

I didn't sleep well that night. I was worried that I had uncovered the reason that this was the city that never slept. The next day was beautiful and sunny, so I shook off my bad first night and headed into Manhattan to run errands, browse through the endless stacks of books at the Strand, and have dinner with Madeleine. It was a perfect New York day, but that night brought back fears of cockroach invasions. My skin was so itchy that I was up half the night listening for roaches and scratching. Now my paranoia had moved on to my ultimate fear—bedbugs. The few hours I did sleep, my feverish dreams had bugs crawling all over me. I missed my roach-free apartment. I missed lying on my sofa watching TV. I missed being able to make myself a nice dinner. The kind of dinner that required pots and pans, herbs and spices, and a fork to shovel it all into my mouth. I had none of that here.

The third night I cried. Not a tiny woe-is-me cry but the kind of giant messy sob fest where you find yourself in front of a mirror just to see how much the hardships of your life have reddened your eyes. The mirror revealed a justifiably puffy tear-streaked face of a person who may have made the biggest mistake of her life.

The days were fine, but the second I set foot back in the apartment, my homesickness awoke with a vengeance. Maybe I wasn't as tough as I'd thought.

I was mistaking myself for the younger me who had slept on bunk beds in Bangkok and peed into holes without a second thought. Now I couldn't even handle a bug or two. I had to get it together. I calmed down and took stock of the situation. I was going to make this work. I was not going home with my tail between my legs. I was a grown woman. Most important, I was way too cheap and now too poor to pay to change my flight.

I recleaned the apartment the next day, finding a storehouse of dust I hadn't previously noticed. I also acknowledged what it was I was really missing.

"I want to buy a TV," I told Madeleine.

"Pardon?"

"I want a TV," I said. "I miss the noise. I miss watching

things. I can buy some DVDs and not sit in silence all the time."

"You moved to New York. There are a million things to do here. And you want to sit and watch TV?"

Madeleine was not a fan of television. She worked in advertising and had once told me that she never watched TV, only the commercials. I told her that was the dumbest thing I had ever heard in my life and to never repeat it in public. Commercials were what allowed you to refill your popcorn bowl and get back to the show without missing anything. What lunacy.

"Yes, I do," I said. "So what? I'm going to be home for an hour or two a day and I don't want to sit in silence. Plus, you know how much I love TV."

When I was a child, I started watching TV as an escape from my uneventful life, but that soon evolved into a love for scripted television. I could sit on a sofa for a full weekend watching a series whose characters and story lines sucked me in.

That night I lugged my new television up the stairs. I had found it online; the seller was a girl who had upgraded her set. It was a full-size TV with DVD player built in for only forty dollars. I had spent more on T-shirts I wore only once, so this was, to me, a great investment.

Then there was the cherry on top. As I passed a street vendor the next day, a case full of DVDs caught my eye.

"That's a great show right there," the vendor said, nodding toward the DVDs. "Classic stuff."

"I know," I said. "I haven't seen it in years."

Ahhh, *Dallas*—my family's Friday-night tradition for most of my childhood. I couldn't resist. When I got home, I popped in a tape and reacquainted myself with the complexities of J. R. and Sue Ellen's relationship and the family dynamics between Bobby, J.R., and Jock. Then there was good old Cliff Barnes.

When my sisters and I missed an episode, my grandmother would watch it for us. Although she spoke no English, she was able to accurately sum up the story for us.

"Then J.R. was with the cheerleader," she would tell us as we listened excitedly. "Sue Ellen slapped him, then the old man fell down a hill." She was better than TiVo and she often added some colorful commentary about J.R.'s indiscretions, complete with a litany of Punjabi swearwords. She did great reviews of many of the shows we liked to watch. She didn't like how short Wonder Woman's shorts were, so called her Bandhar Woman, meaning monkey woman. She felt similarly about the tightness of Superman's eighties aerobics look of thong over Lycra and called him Stupid Man. *Stupid* was one of the English words we felt it important that she learn, so we taught it to her. She really spoke only a few words in English, the most important two used for when she was home alone and the phone rang: NO ENGLISH.

Though Bibi would tsk and wave her hand in the air every time J.R. was with a new woman, every Friday night she was right there alongside the rest of my family to watch the latest episode. Even a grandmother from a rural farming town in India wanted to know just exactly who shot J.R.

As I sat alone in my New York apartment, listening to the

opening theme music of the show, I remembered sitting on the floor in a house full of family, enjoying our Friday-night ritual. I watched a couple of episodes, then drifted off to the sound of the catchy disco-infused theme song. It was the best sleep I had since landing in the city.

→ SEVENTEEN ←

thirty going on thirteen

By the next week, I was in a good frame of mind. I had a phone, I was getting settled into my apartment, and I was looking forward to creating a routine. I joined the local community center, which cost an unheard-of six dollars a month. For that bargain-basement price, you were given access to a steamy weight room and a scalding-hot cardio room where an average of two of the ten machines would be out of service at any given time. One stair climber had a piece of paper taped to it that read "Only Works on Manuel." I kept waiting for this elusive Manuel to come and rouse the exercise machine back to life, but he never showed.

Another important element of getting myself settled was creating a proper space to get some work done. After having worked in the same work space for so many years, I vowed to create a new office for myself.

I had applied for a job blogging for a website aimed at teenagers, and was thrilled when they hired me to be part of the team.

The blog paid enough to give me pocket money for the week, in return for three to four page-length posts about things that mattered to teens. I needed to make some money, but this one was a struggle for me, as I knew nothing of teenagers. I would have liked to use my own experiences in my writing, but I didn't think I would get much traction with posts like "the best haircuts to mask sideburns" or "one pair of jeans, thirty ways."

It would be a challenge to be the voice of a phase of life that I'd wished would end immediately when I was going through it. I spent most of my teenage years with a mustache that I thought was invisible because I had bleached it fluorescent yellow. I worked the early shift at a doughnut shop just to buy myself the same cotton khakis the other girls wore and so I would have an excuse for why I couldn't go out on the weekends. This blog job would be an exercise in creative writing, as I had a feeling mine weren't the most common of teenage experiences.

Packing up my laptop and an equal-size bag of snacks, I took the L train into town, got off at Bryant Park, and walked up the imposing stone stairs of my new daytime refuge. On either side of me, large stone lions kept watch over the building. What more majestic place for a mind to wander than the New York Public Library? There were countless rooms of lovely long tables at which to create masterpieces while surreptitiously shoving licorice whips into your mouth.

I set up my workstation, and after mindlessly surfing the net for a while, I finally got down to work. But what to say? I hadn't the slightest idea where to begin. I hadn't been a teenager for over a decade and so much had changed in that time. I didn't have a computer with an Internet provider until I was in college, and even there, I didn't have a cell phone. I was a nerd of a teenager, and not much had changed, except that I now wore contacts, not glasses, when I sat down for my daily hour of *Star Trek*.

Each day I took the subway into town, walked to Fifth Avenue, and headed back to my office. Each day I would struggle to come up with topics, doing research by reading other teen blogs and watching the cringe-inducing reality shows that were popular with teens. But the work paid, and this was key.

I wanted to keep busy and take some lessons in New York. Although I was moving very slowly but surely in everything I had come to the city to do, I knew that there was a chance that living here would distract me from my goal and I sometimes found myself wanting to go to a gallery, museum, or show instead of getting down to work. What I loved about New York was unfortunately going to mean that I wouldn't be able to get anything done. With little money in my entertainment budget, I would just head home every night and eat my dinner in front of the television, watching episodes of *Dallas*.

I wasn't exactly living a life out of *Sex and the City,* a show that wants you to believe that people who are lawyers or own PR firms have time for drinks every night (and that writers who drop a pun into every single conversation *don't* get punched out by their girlfriends). In reality, most everyone I knew in New York worked relentless hours to allow them to live in New York. It was the Manhattan catch-22.

Nonetheless, the lack of social engagements allowed me more time to get down to the task at hand. In my second week, I popped into the Fourteenth Street YMCA and signed up for swimming before I changed my mind.

I had planned to sign up for a group swimming class but had missed the deadlines for all of them. Not wanting to chicken out, I decided that I would cough up the dough and sign up for private swimming lessons. This was a life skill that I needed to learn. It would be worth dipping into my pocket further than I had expected.

I had some income coming in from my teen-blog gig, so I allowed myself the indulgence. The trouble was, I was finding it increasingly difficult to brainstorm topics for a teenage audience.

I would surf *Tiger Beat* and *Teen Vogue* and various other publications that I could have a daughter old enough to read and desperately tried to come up with topics.

"What about back-to-school shopping with your parents?" I would suggest to my editor. "Or how to dress straight out of *Gossip Girl*?"

Invariably, the topic I knew least about would be chosen and I would sit down to watch *Gossip Girl* so I could actually differentiate Blair from Serena.

My first few posts were sent back to me three times each for revisions.

"Make them funnier!" I was told. "Make them more relatable and really try to capture the voice of youth." I didn't have the voice of youth even when I was one myself, so this was challenging. I continued to rework the pieces until they were finally accepted. The third entry, an opus that focused on the biting teen debate about whether it's better to date a vampire or a werewolf, I wrote in ten minutes. It was declared a literary triumph.

From that point on, I stopped trying to write as me and inserted "LOL!" and "OMG!" until I could no longer respect myself.

"Who else is sick for the Jonas boys?!" I wrote, having heard of them only the day before. "Have you ever IM'd the wrong crush? Were you totally grossed out when your mom joined Facebook? How else can the 'rents embarrass you?!" "TOTALLY!" my audience replied. "Isn't that the worst?" Personally, the worst for me was sounding like a girl with a backstage pass for a Miley Cyrus concert.

The more I talked about topics that I hated and inserted a variety of popular phrases that were shredding the English language to bits, the better received was my writing.

I was writing pieces on subjects I knew nothing about. I actually wrote a post on summer romances: "Danny and Sandy really summed it up in *Grease,* didn't they? Nothing adds to the joy of vacation like summer love." Little did the readers know that I was referring to the one-sided romance I had growing up, with Lucky on *General Hospital*. I wrote about loving the *Twilight* film (which I didn't even see) and how LOLish it was when you and your BFF are crushing on the same guy. I wanted to strangle this teen me I had created.

It turned out that pretty quickly the readers wanted to strangle me back. I made a very large mistake. A mistake so large that it rocked the world of teen blogging as we know it: I wrote a post on the most sacred of tween/teen literature: Harry Potter books. And it was factually incorrect.

The pieces I wrote were meant to be humorous, so I wrote jokes about a number of characters, including one that apparently dies in one of the last books in the series. Why didn't anybody tell me that Dumbledore died! Aren't wizards supposed to live forever? Gandalf returned for the end of *Lord of the Rings,* so why couldn't the Harry Potter readers have faith that Dumbledore could show up for the Hogwarts graduation? I can admit it; I had totally screwed up. The comments linked to the post were nothing short of an online burning at the stake.

"This writer should be ashamed of herself!" one teen wrote. I was mortified but at least thankful they could tell I was a female.

"DUH!" another kid wrote. "DUMBLEDORE IS DEAD!"

"Thousands of people are laughing at you!" another chimed in. I wasn't sure this was true but I was pretty sure that my next post should be about the horrors of cyberbullying. In my day, they just yelled "Nice unibrow, Rupinder!" while you waited in line for the drinking fountain, but now they were taking to the Internet to tear you down.

Not all of the comments were negative, especially a particularly kind one from CatLover4Ever (i.e., Jen), who proclaimed the entry to be genius. But there were enough negative comments to cause me to run home from the library worried that a mob of kids had traced my IP address and would come after me wielding Quidditch brooms.

I wondered if perhaps the slip had been subconscious, because I had contemplated resigning from this job for a few weeks. A writer needs to learn to write in different voices, it's true, but I realized a few weeks in that I might never master the voice of a North American teenager.

When my editor moved on from her position, another one took over and sent me an e-mail saying that I "wasn't really capturing their voice" and that they didn't need me anymore. I was upset that my sole income was now gone, but it was a small price to pay, in the grand scheme of things. Some things in life you don't want to relive. Teenage rejection is one of them.

EIGHTEEN

curbed enthusiasm

Settling into New York was taking a lot longer than I had expected. My building was generally quiet, but twice I was awakened in the dead of the night by a girl leaving her boyfriend's apartment.

"You must think I'm crazy!" she would scream, voicing her disapproval of whatever he had done to irk her that night.

He would yell at her to stay, she would yell back an expletive-laced tirade, and the whole building would be robbed of that night's sleep.

I didn't find many of the neighbors that friendly, either. I had left notes for three neighbors on my floor, asking if they would want to split their Internet with me for the duration of my stay. All three completely ignored me, even when I saw them in the hall.

On the other end of the spectrum, the neighbors two doors down from me had an extremely liberal open-door policy. In the same basic four-hundred-square-foot apartment I was renting, a family of at least five had created a home. Each time I passed, the door was open, allowing me a glimpse of plastic tablecloth, an earful of yelling in Spanish, and a delicious whiff of that day's lunch or dinner. As the washing machine constantly whirred, a middle-aged woman stood above the steamy stove, delicious scents of chalupas wafting out to tease me as I headed to my apartment to eat my third grilled-cheese dinner of the week. We never really stopped to talk but I would smile at whomever's eye I caught as I passed. They didn't seem to care who snuck a peek into their private lives.

In my memories, the two-bedroom apartment that my extended family and I all lived in was five times the size of this one, but I wondered if that was true. If you just exchanged some of the smells of corn flour with that of paprika, their situation was very similar to my life twenty-seven years ago. The biggest difference being that my family always kept the door closed, to hide our overpopulated situation, whereas this family wasn't at all self-conscious.

One day, as I stumbled up the stairs with my bags of groceries, I looked up and my gaze went directly into their apartment, where a little girl was in the bathroom, sitting on the toilet. She looked me straight in the eye.

As her mother yelled, "Maria, don't we close the door when we go to the bathroom?" the girl kept staring. No blinks. No turning away. I accepted her challenge, walking slowly up the stairs while my eyes started tearing from the trauma of not blinking. I was the new person on the floor and I had to assert myself and claim my space. She was unflinching. I am not sure who won the stare-off. I held my own but she was staring while not wearing underwear, and anyone worth their staring salt knows that gives you an extra five points.

As I wondered what the rest of the building thought of this family, I began to wonder as well what our building had thought of my own, a family of nine living in a two-bedroom apartment. Perhaps people had thought that we were unfortunate to be living in such cramped quarters, because my parents were new to the country, doing what they could to create solid beginnings for themselves. This family was likely doing the same thing, and after they moved onward and upward, another new family would take their place. They always said hello to me as I walked by, and waved to me when they saw me in the lobby. They reminded me of my family when we lived in the apartment building, poor but happy. I wondered if Maria had a grandmother to watch her TV shows for her.

There was another factor that made me wonder if I was going to last in the big city. You know there is something wrong when you are bored in New York City. But I was. I was utterly bored some days and mildly bored for parts of others. I would wake up late, wonder how I would spend my day, and be in bed by ten, ready to repeat the process again the next day. I wanted to slap myself for thinking it, but maybe I was a bit lost without a job, and perhaps I should have been clearer with myself as to what my dreams were. It was evident, later than would have been useful, that I didn't want to just *live* in New York, I wanted to have a *life* in New York.

I wanted a job I loved, a great apartment, and the ability to do whatever I wanted. I guess that is why it's a dream. Because reality is boredom during the days when you work and extreme boredom during the days when you don't. It's realizing that the comedy show costs money and that you have nobody to see it with and that you are not a New Yorker but a tourist with an extremely poorly planned itinerary. And worse, that you are a cliché: a starry-eyed bumpkin who had come to make it in the city, and didn't know where to begin.

→ NINETEEN ←

diff'rent strokes

After registering at the Y near Union Square, I made an appointment to see my swimming instructor, Freddie, for the first time on a Wednesday afternoon. The week before the lesson, I lost my nerve and tried to think of a reason to cancel. I wanted to know how to swim but I did not want to get into the water and learn how to swim in the same way that people you see on reality shows want to be singers but never bother to take a voice lesson. My days became occupied with looking for excuses not to attend. But Monday, Freddie called to confirm the appointment and I was locked in.

The day before the lesson, I went in search of a swimsuit. I didn't have an Internet connection at the apartment, so I often stumbled out into the city blindly, hoping for kind strangers to refer me to the particular service or location I required. With this strategy in mind, I started off at a Kmart, where I tested out a series of towels that I made sure wrapped around my whole body. "Excuse me," I said to a salesgirl nearby. "Do you sell bathing suits here?"

"Mmm, uh-uh, honey," she said, shaking her head. "It ain't the summer." Apparently bathing suits now went by the same rules that forbid white after Labor Day. No doubt Michael Phelps would top the fall Worst Dressed lists. I wanted to ask her where I would be able to find one, but she had already walked away to tackle the very important task of folding washcloths.

"Excuse me," I said to the next salesgirl I encountered. "Do you know where there's a sporting-goods store around here?"

"Oh, sorry," she said. "I don't live around here."

"But you work here," I replied. "Have you seen any in the area?"

"No," she said, looking away. I asked several other salespeople, but nobody else seemed to have seen any stores in the area either, making me wonder whether Kmart was so competitive that its workers were trained never to offer the name of a rival, or whether the Kmart employees were bussed in every day wearing blindfolds designed by Jaclyn Smith.

The security guard at least offered me a general direction to walk in and I headed back toward Union Square. There, a helpful yoga-store employee pointed me in the right direction and I was soon in a sporting-goods store, staring bleakly at a rack of bathing suits.

Drowning while trying to learn a whip kick or being seen in a bathing suit: I didn't know which possibility frightened me more at the time. I gathered eight suits, holding them in my hand with such disdain one would think they were flaming bags of dog excrement. I headed into the changing room, hoping for a miracle.

The first one sandwiched my breasts so they were nearly spilling out the armholes and the second one had them almost spilling out of the leg holes. Each and every one accentuated the negative and made my legs look like two sausage links that had been crammed into the suit. I was in the changing room for at least an hour, discarding five suits, then crying and begging the remaining three to please cut me some slack and about four inches off both of my thighs.

"Just yell if you need any help," said the salesgirl, who, though pregnant, had a smaller stomach than I did. The issue for me was that my problem areas were pretty much everywhere that the suit didn't cover, which I would normally shield from the innocent eyes of bystanders. I tried on the last three suits four more times each. Each one had a different problem. Only when I noticed that two of the suits were exactly the same did I resign myself to the realization that this was a losing battle. I picked up the last suit and headed for the cash register.

"I also need some goggles and a swim cap," I told the man at the counter.

"Okay," he said, pointing out some options. "These should work."

I took my purchases home immediately and donned the bathing suit and swim cap before giving up on the goggles. Despite my efforts, I had lost no inches or pounds on the walk home. I just had to get used to the thought that I would be almost completely exposed in front of strangers. I walked around the apartment in the suit and cap. Pausing for a drink in the kitchen, I looked out the window to see a neighbor peering in curiously. I waved and smiled, as if to make him believe that I was aware of a secret pool in the building of which he had not been informed, then walked into my bedroom and collapsed on the bed.

The first day of swimming had finally arrived. I showed up at the Y early, having arranged to meet my Freddie at 2 P.M. The pool had a giant glass wall on one side so people could sit in the lobby and watch their kids or just stare into the water's calm reflection after their Pilates class. I had a few minutes and I sat and watched an Indian woman, who looked a few years my senior, taking a private lesson. If she can do it, I can do it, I thought. But the more I looked at the Olympic-size pool, the more I didn't want to do it. Water, swirling. In mouth. In nose. In lungs. Life over. Swimming really wasn't *that* important. I was happy to just hang out on the beach during vacations. Really, it was where the true action was. I would get one of those metal detectors and look for coins or perfect my sand-castle-building technique. Cruise ships were overrated and, at pool parties, nobody is swimming a fifty-meter breaststroke. As long as I could hang out, sans bathing suit, on the pool deck and look good, that was enough. Yes, I had better leave and head off to the gym instead.

Don't be an idiot, the voice in my head snapped. *You've paid for this, you're doing it.* The voice in my head always appealed to the Indian frugality in me. After quitting my job, I was living out the rest of the year on a budget and could not spend hundreds of dollars on a suit and lessons that I was going to abandon. Sigh. I tried to offer myself the whatever-doesn't-kill-me-makes-me-stronger mantra; then it occurred to me that if my instructor looked away for a second to pinch his bathing-suit wedgie, this *could* potentially kill me. I headed for an exit, but then I imagined poor Freddie, hanging out in the chilly pool alone, searching for me in the bathing-suited crowd. I grudgingly headed for the locker room.

I changed like I was Dustin Hoffman in *Tootsie,* surreptitiously hiding from the other women. Under my dress, I pulled off the underwear and pulled on the bathing suit. A towel quickly wrapped itself around my lower half. Then the dress came off while the bathing suit simultaneously went on in its place. And with that, I headed to the showers. My swim cap looked like a latex hairnet, lumpily pulling together my mane, parts of which still peeked out of the sides. After a mandatory shower, I headed out into the unknown, the strange land called the swimming pool. The lady in the lesson before mine was just finishing up when I arrived. She patted herself dry and I announced, "I'm up next. I'm learning to swim, too." She smiled and wished me well, a slight British accent in her voice.

"Are you Rupinder?" Freddie asked from the pool. His bright yellow swim cap gave him the appearance of an aquatic Chiquita Banana.

I nodded and moved forward. Throwing my towel onto a bench, I eased myself cautiously down the stairs into the tepid water.

He shook my hand and I thrust my goggles into his palm. "How do I put these on?" I asked. Freddie was likely a decade younger than I was, but because he could swim, he was my poolside Yoda.

He took the goggles from my hand, and while I held them over my eyes, he struggled to secure them in place.

"Wow, you have a lot of hair under there," he said while stretching the rubber strap as far as the laws of physics would allow.

I sure hoped he was talking about my swim cap.

"How's that?" he asked while snapping it in place.

"It feels quite tight," I admitted. My eyes felt as if they were squished into an ophthalmological girdle, but Freddie assured me that this would work for the time being.

"Okay," he announced. "Why don't you show me what you can do."

I looked at the water, adjusted my foot position slightly, put my arms out a little farther in front of me, then rotated them clockwise to create a minuscule ripple in the water. Putting them back at my sides, I shrugged. "Well, I think that's the extent of it." We both laughed.

"Don't worry," he assured me. "We'll take this slow."

For the first ten minutes, we practiced simply walking in the water, submerged to shoulder level. Like chlorine-addicted zombies, we walked with our arms outstretched back and forth, back and forth, half the length of a lane. Even this was proving to be an Olympic-level challenge for me. After five steps, I would feel myself swerving toward the wall, the sixth step forcing me to careen into it. After my path straightened out, Freddie said something alarming. We were going to now put our faces in the water.

Hold your water horses. I did not sign up for this. I didn't sign up to lose my oxygen and gain a panic attack in the closed swimming-pool lane of the West Village Y. I know it sounds cowardly, but adults are cowards. Seven-year-olds are not afraid of swimming. They haven't seen *The Poseidon Adventure* and other disaster-at-sea films, so are not yet aware that water submersion and breathing are the oil and water of the survival world. I had nightmares for weeks after watching *Titanic,* though in fairness, some of that was due to Billy Zane's eyebrows. Kids think that like their age-appropriate frame of reference, the heroine of *The Little Mermaid,* they can survive underwater indefinitely and sing songs of merriment with creatures of the sea.

"Walk five steps and take a deep breath and put your whole head in," Freddie instructed.

He wasn't going to let me off the hook. Okay, I said silently. Easy does it. You can do this. I walked five steps, looked over at him, then walked another two, followed by another one before I gulped in a copious amount of oxygen and plunged my head beneath the depths.

"Great!" Freddie said as I emerged one nanosecond later. "But I should tell you that you don't need to close your eyes under there if you're wearing goggles."

I was already learning so much

After another fifteen minutes of doing five steps then submersion, I was keeping my eyes open but was still concerned about the water that would fill my nose and mouth at any given moment. Freddie's attempts at teaching me to exhale underwater resulted simply in my exiting the water each time I needed a fresh breath. "You need to stay down there longer," Freddie cautioned. "Hold your breath as long as you can."

That was exactly what I was doing. Take a breath, go underwater, count to three, and come back up. Three seconds seemed reasonable to me. There wasn't a coral reef, or a sneak preview of the newest Scorsese film down there. What was I staying down there to see?

"Now hold your breath, go under, and float as long as you can," Freddie said, upping the ante. "Exhale underwater. I want to see some bubbles."

"How long are these lessons?" I asked, looking at the clock. I knew perfectly well that they were a half hour, and knowing that we had mutually decided on an end was making it easier for me.

"Oh, don't worry," Freddie said. "I'm happy to keep going." Damn him for being interested in my personal growth.

I had wasted a lot of time both in the pool and in life. It was my method of stalling so I didn't have to commit to anything too deeply. But if Freddie could be committed to ensuring that a perfect stranger learned to swim, I needed to honor my commitment to the task myself.

"Oh, thanks," I said, adjusting my goggles. "That's great."

"Sure," Freddie said. "Now go ahead and float."

Okay, deep breath. I was going to go for it. I pulled in a breath so big it could have ripped Dorothy's house from the Kansas soil and I plunged my head underwater. Then I floated. Then I kicked a bit. My God, was I swimming? I think I was swimming! I wouldn't be racing Michael Phelps anytime soon but I was now at least a contender.

Bubbles, bubbles, bubbles. Hold on a bit longer. Keep going. Now stand up. Mission accomplished.

"I'm proud of you!" Freddie proclaimed when I touched the wall. "You did it!"

I did it! How truly insane that I thought I would live my

life without ever doing something so simple, so rudimentary. Before this year, being a nonswimmer was just my reality. I was convinced that I was never going to learn to swim. My mom couldn't swim and would likely never learn. I couldn't think of one single female relative over thirty who could swim. My sisters couldn't swim either, although I hoped that they would one day also give it a try. If we capsized on a family boat cruise tomorrow, my dad and brother would have to exhaust themselves in the rescue effort while we flailed around the water.

Afterward, I truly felt I had accomplished something. Freddie shook my hand at the end of the lesson and reiterated how proud he was of me. This may not seem like a big deal to some, but the nonswimmers out there know the crippling fears and emotions that are keeping them out of the water. Swimming frightened me more than bungee jumping, skydiving, and bullfighting all wrapped into one. So to me, it was a big deal. No, it was an enormous deal.

In the locker room, a glimpse in the mirror revealed deep-set rings around my eyes, caused by the suction of my goggles. I tried to rub them out and pinch the skin back to its regular plumpness. The sauna was right behind me, so I decided to wait out the recovery in the soothing heat.

When I opened the door, I was greeted by a fully naked geriatric woman lying on a bench. Her legs were in the air, doing some sort of X-rated air bicycling. Her privates became uncomfortably public with each and every casual pedal. As if steaming herself, putting on a peep show, and doing calisthenics was not challenge enough, she also multitasked in the loofahing of her heels. Moving past her, I took a seat in the corner of the opposite bench and arranged my towels to create a perfect cushy base. I had already stripped down to a bathing suit in public, which was considered by Indian modesty standards to be a step below twirling around a stripper pole. I didn't imagine I would ever get to the point of being able to handle full public nudity. At least not today.

Closing my eyes, I relished the heat swirling around me. I wrung my hair out into a towel and let the warmth pull the smell of chlorine off my skin. What a wonderful feeling. When I opened my eyes, my sauna mate was sitting up and had moved on to rubbing lotion all over her freshly toned and scrubbed body. Feeling fully refreshed, I ran my fingers around my eyes and noticed that the dents had subsided considerably, so I was ready to join the general public again.

After I showered and changed, I wandered out into the hallway. Through the glass from the pool lobby, I spotted a group of kindergarten-age kids on the pool deck ready for their lessons. They all wore tiny swim caps and some had goggles already in place. Their mothers were on the benches in front of me, watching them. Some of them looked younger than me and were beautifully dressed and manicured, in the way of Manhattan women who are free at three in the afternoon. I stepped out into the September afternoon sunshine to catch my train home.

By the second lesson you'd think that my fears would have diminished. The day before the lesson was scheduled, I tried to think of a reason to cancel. The morning of the lesson, I still had butterflies in my stomach. I picked up the phone to call Freddie and saw that the battery was dead. Fate was telling me to stop being a baby.

When I walked down the stairs to the pool, I was fifteen minutes early, so I took a seat in the pool lobby to watch through the glass. The woman from last week was finishing up her lesson. She was already in the deep end. Dear Lord, I was not ready for that. I was not ready for that at all. How did she get so far ahead of me? I cursed myself for not practicing, but the pool near where I lived was so small and was overrun by a clique of Orthodox Jewish women who dominated the dressing room and filled the pool at maximum capacity every time I was there.

I went and got changed, feeling a lot more comfortable with the cap, goggles, and shower routine already.

I took a seat on a bench on the pool deck just as the woman was emerging from the water. "Wow," I said. "You're doing great. Which lesson are you on?"

"The third," she said. "I think I'm getting the hang of it."

Okay, she was one lesson ahead of me. In swimming terms, that was like the difference between an undergraduate degree and a PhD. I would no longer compare myself to her. She was too experienced for comparison.

"Hi again." Freddie waved from the pool. I folded my towel, left it on the bench, and joined him the water.

"I think I've forgotten everything," I admitted.

"Don't worry," he said. "We'll start again."

And we did. Back to zombie walks. Then faces in water. On to gliding.

After twenty minutes, Freddie said, "You seem to really hesitate when you're underwater."

"I know," I apologized. "I just don't know what it is. It's completely a mental issue."

"Come over to the wall," he said. "You're going to stand here, go under, and hold your breath for as long as possible. Let's start with ten seconds."

Start with? That seemed like an eternity to me. People ran the hundred-yard dash in less time.

Plunging my head under, I listened to Freddie's voice coming from above the water. "Eight . . . nine . . . ten.

"Great work!" he said as I wiped the water from my goggles. "I'm so proud of you! Now try twenty."

Twenty seconds. No oxygen. This was frightening. I imagined Freddie standing trial for my murder. The thought of photos of me in my bathing suit being passed around in a courtroom made me vow to conquer the challenge.

Deep breath. Head under. Freddie's voice beckoned from above. "Five . . . six . . . seven . . ." *Don't think about it. You have plenty of air.* "Eleven . . . twelve . . ." *More than halfway done, stay calm.* ". . . Sixteen . . . nineteen . . . twenty.

"You did it!" he yelled as I swallowed in every last drop of air.

"You'd better not say 'thirty' now," I said, wiping water from my goggles.

He laughed and gave me a high five as people in the lane beside us looked on.

"Listen," he said. "I appreciate how willing you are. I can see that you're scared and yet you do everything I ask."

"Well, thank you for being so patient," I replied. "I'll try to practice. I have to."

After showering and changing, I sat on the bench in the

pool lobby for a while, watching the next set of lessons. Wow, those five-year-olds were good. With such reckless abandon they jumped into the pool, unaware of and uninterested in the depth of the water. Their parents all sat cheering them on and holding their teddy bears as they swam.

As I watched the kids with envy, I noticed a Speedo-clad man on the pool deck walk over to the glass wall. He knocked on it and waved to catch my attention. When I looked up, he gave me a big smile and a thumbs-up. I laughed and waved back as everyone looked over at me. I guess I had some cheerleaders, too.

After the lesson, Melissa and I met for what ended up being a media networking event at the über-cool Bedford Bowl bowling alley in Brooklyn. It was a giant complex of neon-lit lanes, flanked with rich leather sofas. At the back of the room was a giant modern bar and standing around it were dozens of people wearing name tags. "Eric, Fashion," one read. "Louise, Fusion Design," said the name tag of a beautiful black girl in a zebra-print dress and stiletto boots. "Oh, man," I said to Mel. "I don't know about the name tags."

"Rupinder, Tap Dancer." "Rupinder, Unemployed." "Rupinder, Insane." I hated the what-do-you-do-for-a-living conversation.

This stemmed from my struggle to get to the point of wearing the illustrious name tag of "Rupinder, TV Publicist."

Before that job, I worked a slew of terrible ones, freelancing and interning and doing whatever I had to on the side in hopes of landing a job in my field. During the day, I took abuse from people on the phone; I lost a permanent job to a kid who didn't even graduate high school, entered data, and entered incredible depression. Once, after a particularly disheartening temp job where I found myself putting out drinks and sandwiches at an accounting firm, I cried on the subway ride home. It was a pleasant enough place to work. Senior staff came by to shake my hand and welcome me. But I had gone to school for five years and was putting out fruit salads for kids younger than me who had professional jobs. As subway onlookers peered over uncomfortably, I sat in my seat and cried, seeing no way out of toiling in unskilled labor forever.

But during those days, which were financially difficult, dark, depressing, and sobering all at the same time, I never felt like I was "Rupinder, Telemarketer" or "Rupinder, Office Temp." I couldn't, because defining myself that way made me feel like it was going to be my reality forever.

Besides, the North American obsession with work always struck me as overrated. But that was an argument admittedly weakened by the fact that I didn't work at all. Which, in the crowd of movers and shakers I found myself among at the moment, would be tantamount to wearing the name tag of "Rupinder, Huge Nobody."

"What's the problem?" Melissa asked, seeing the look on my face.

"I don't always love networking events," I said.

"Me neither," she said. "Let's just stay for ten minutes and see what we think," she said, walking over to the bar.

"The other thing is, what *do* I do, Mel?" I asked her.

We turned down the offer of name tags and went to get some sushi.

"You're so hard on yourself," she said. "You're *going* to do great things."

Melissa was always skilled at pep talks, something I found myself needing since I landed in New York.

"I just don't know where my life is headed anymore," I admitted. "And sometimes I wonder if coming to New York was a mistake. It's cool and it's great, but it doesn't feel like home, and well, it's kind of lonely."

In fact, my biggest shock in New York was not the Latin lovers in my neighborhood, who catcalled to me each and every time I passed, or how well the subway system retained the smell of urine each day. It was that after nearly a month, I was still lonely. In New York City, for God's sake! In the city that never sleeps, I slept ten hours every night, at a loss for how to fill my day.

"When I first moved here, I was so depressed," Melissa confessed. "I didn't have friends, I had nothing to do, I didn't have my own life, and I felt like I wasn't in control. I would sleep until noon or just make up errands to do. It took me at least four months to feel settled."

"But you had Ken. That must have made things tolerable. And unfortunately I don't have that much time," I said.

It is one thing to be lonely but another to be lonely and poor. Having been raised to be cautious with money, I started to feel sick to my stomach at the rent I was paying, the price of a meal, the price of a grocery-store sandwich when you are trying to avoid going out for a meal, and the general cost of life. Most of my friends in the city had jobs with great salaries, and though they weren't extravagant people, I could never help but feel like I was bringing down the fun by always saying no to meals and shopping and the things I used to enjoy once upon a time. I was starting to not enjoy anything and thus was making my experience the exact opposite of what I had set out for it to be.

The cost of leaving a comfortable life was difficult. I always thought of myself as adventurous. On my first day at college, I was up at 7 A.M., packed and ready to head out for a new life in a new city. But here in New York, without classes to distract me or a residence full of two hundred other women I had yet to meet, I was bored. When I was eighteen, I relished the thought of university, knowing I was leaving my old life and inventing a new one for myself. Now, past thirty, I had abandoned that life on what felt like a whim.

In truth, I realize that I had felt this at home as well. It wasn't necessarily loneliness but the general aimlessness of not knowing where your life is heading. But these feelings were amplified tenfold in a place where I had no job, no routine, no money, and a void of the familiar faces that would normally fill my day. I had none of my creature comforts, the things that wonderfully distract normal people from having to fully realize the true mundaneness of their normalcy.

→ TWENTY ←

blind date

Perhaps sensing that I was looking for ways to fill my time, a friend set me up on a date. With an Indian girl. This was in ways vastly more important than my being set up with a man, because I did not have one single Indian friend (ever). When I was growing up, this was strictly a supply-and-demand issue. There was neither supply nor demand. Indians always seemed to travel in packs, which was not all that strange, as a lot of people have groups of friends of their same culture. I was never in such a pack. But as an adult, I realized the advantages that having some Indian friends would offer, like being able to be honest about how strict my parents were and sharing the experience of navigating two cultures unsuccessfully.

So when my friend suggested that I meet Natasha, I sent her an e-mail and planned a date. New York, city of transients and transplants, can often bring out the friendliness in people. When you are new to the city, you are desperate for human contact, and once you are settled in the city, you recall those preliminary feelings and take hosting duties to heart. Dinner invitations are offered, maps drawn, names of contacts and associates freely given.

Natasha e-mailed that she was heading to a seminar at the New York Television Festival and asked if I would like to join her.

"Yes, absolutely!" I typed. "I'm a television publicist by day, so would love to check it out."

After I hit SEND, I realized that I was not actually a television publicist anymore. A simple slip of the mind. I was now a full-time bum. But at least by meeting Natasha I was making a first step into investigating whether the creative side of TV was for me.

She and I agreed to meet on the corner of Fifty-first and Seventh Avenue to have dinner before the seminar. I was fifteen minutes early, of course, so I had to stand outside and fight the crowds streaming up from Times Square. Directly to my north stood the studio where they shoot *The Late Show with David Letterman*. When I was living back in my parents' basement after graduating from college, I once submitted a joke to the show's online top-ten list as a lark. It made it on the list and I received an XL *Late Show* T-shirt as a prize. It was the highlight of that year for me.

I scanned the flood of people for Natasha. I knew only that she was Indian, so was forced to smile at every Indian, olive-skinned, or Hare Krishna woman that passed by me. After five minutes, I saw a pretty young girl walk into the coffee shop and scan the crowd. I smiled at her and she waved and came outside.

"Rupinder," she said, greeting me with a hug. "Welcome."

She was like a tiny Indian Barbie doll, with beautiful olive skin and giant Princess Jasmine eyes. She outlined all of our dinner choices and we finally agreed to go to Ellen's Stardust Diner, a purported favorite among theater-going tourists. We walked into the diner, which was all decked out fifties-style. The waitresses wore poodle skirts and had name tags with ridiculous monikers like P-Nut and Fancy. The waiters were all made up to look like a cross between Richie Cunningham and the Fonz.

We sat down and I said to Natasha, "So you're originally from Canada as well?"

She nodded and launched into her story, which was cut off after the third word by a chorus of waitresses singing "Mamma Mia." I looked around, confused. The cliché of waiters who really want to be actors seemed to be built into the business plan of the restaurant. While diners munched on oversize sandwiches, the team of waiters and waitresses took turns singing show tunes and dancing from table to table. "Here we go again . . ." sang one perpetually smiling waitress, her arm around a giggling middle-aged German man with a camera slung around his neck. As the musical stylings continued, loud enough no doubt to be heard on Broadway itself, Natasha and I leaned in and yelled to each other in an effort to trade our stories of Indian upbringings.

"How long have you been here?" I asked, relishing the greasy goodness of my chicken fingers.

"I was here last year for a six-month trial period," she said, "but then, of course, I went back home."

Of course. The feelings of homesicknesses were definitely starting to subside. I could see myself staying in New York and enjoying it. And it was inspiring, in the way that jealousy can be inspiring, to meet someone who was pretty much a younger version of me, but had beat me to everything.

I told her of a writer I wanted to meet but who had not yet responded to my e-mail.

"You'll soon learn," she said, "that people here do what they have to do to get what they want. E-mail again."

I had always cringed at the word *networking* and was not a person who was willing to risk personal humiliation to get somewhere, but when I thought about it some more, I realized that risking everything, including humiliation, was the path that had brought me to this point. I needed to learn how to put myself out there. As a publicist, I had always been great at pushing the newest shows or talent, but doing that exercise for myself was a wholly different proposition.

We walked over to the building where the seminar was taking place. She told me about her dating life. Her parents were aware that she dated but still preferred to avoid the topic. She asked me how I handled the issue with my parents and I told her that under no circumstances would we ever have discussed dating. We had a stricter don't-ask, don't-tell policy than the U.S. military.

As we waited for the elevator doors to open, Natasha turned to me. "Can I ask you something personal and can you be honest?"

"Sure," I said.

"How would you feel about having a boyfriend who wants to go back to school at our age?"

I knew why she asked the question. For an Indian parent, financial stability is the bedrock of a successful marriage, while a man who is a debt-ridden student is more a pool of quicksand.

Natasha was much closer to her parents than I was to mine. Partially because the emotional tie never seemed that solid to begin with, my connection to my parents loosened a bit each year. It was the freedom that this situation allowed me that made it easier for me to make my own choices, even if they were as ridiculous as quitting a steady job to be a kid again for a year.

Natasha clearly cared about her parents' preferences. She reminded me a lot of Gurpreet, who, as the eldest child, always felt it was her burden to respect our parents' wishes. She thought that if she did what they demanded, no matter how unreasonable, they would like her. This led to some fights between us growing up, as the few times a year I did try to go out, she seemed to side with my parents that it would bring a pox upon their house. I always thought she was simply upset that she didn't have the wherewithal to just oppose them and go out herself.

During the question-and-answer period of the seminar, a man stood up to say that he had bought the rights to a story and wanted tips on finding financing for it. The room was full of would-be writers and producers looking to join the glitterati. I wondered if any of them would make it, including myself. I was already in this world, but only as a supporting player. This seminar was about being in the limelight.

"Excuse me," Natasha said, tapping the man on the shoulder when the seminar was done. "What's your background?"

He mentioned that he was Indian, and like an old Indian man finding a fellow villager in a foreign land, she nodded and leaned in to talk further.

"You should contact so-and-so," she said. "Also, try the government grants." She wrote him a list of leads as he thanked her profusely.

"Wow," I said. "You're so nice." And she was. But what really struck me was that she was Indian and very, very comfortable with it. She went out of her way to help this man simply because he too was Indian. During my adolescence, my increasingly cynical views about Indian life had erected a wall of silence between most Indians that crossed my path and me. Now, as an adult, I felt like I would be judged for how culturally unaware I had been for most of my life. Though I still felt like an outsider in my own culture, I was approaching a point where I wanted to just shape my own view and identity.

As I rode the E train downtown toward Brooklyn, I thought about Natasha again. My attitude toward Indians was mostly shaped around what my parents believed a good Indian to be. But in this, I realized that I was the one who missed out. I could not cook curries any better than my white friends. They could probably out-Bhangra me, and any teen *Jeopardy!* contestant would pulverize me on my Indian trivia. With this, I sent out a note to my NYC friends: "We're having an Indian night," I proclaimed. "All Indian, all night long." My parents would be so proud/horrified.

I had been thinking a lot about my parents during my time in New York. Since I left home, they always accused me of never calling them. It was mostly because we always had the same conversation when I did. My dad would ask me how I was, I would ask back, and then there would be an awkward lull. My mom and I would exchange those same pleasantries and then she would ask me if I had eaten, and if so, what I had eaten. It was all very deep and meaningful conversation.

But when I was living in New York, I actually called home a few times, mostly to try to convince my mom to come visit me.

My parents hadn't had much to say about my move to New York. What could they say to me at thirty-one? Besides, they thought I would soon come to my senses, return, and go back to work. Before I left, my mom actually expressed an interest in seeing the city herself for the first time in her life, and I encouraged her to do so. My dad had traveled there with some other Indian men and relatives during the city's peak crime period of the early eighties, but a group of Indian women would never do the same. It simply wasn't done.

Visiting your daughter *was* done, but my mom always had a reason against it. She wanted to, she said, "but I can't walk around there." Five children and a lifetime of manual-labor jobs had taken their toll on her bones. She couldn't walk very far or climb stairs without strain. Her legs and feet were covered in the veins that drove me to the gym, in hopes of avoiding them. I offered to rent us a hotel room and was looking forward to stealing all their soaps, but she balked at the thought of spending the money.

Hoping to change her mind, I researched all of the tourist attractions in the city that didn't require a vast amount of walking and told her that we could do bus tours, take cabs, and make it an experience that would delight her senses but spare her legs. She left me a message on my phone every few days over the next two weeks until I e-mailed my sister and told her to pass on the fact that I only had a phone for emergencies and couldn't use up the minutes. But after feeling guilty, I added more money to it and dialed our home number.

My dad, who was always quick on the call-display draw, picked up.

"Hi, Dad," I said. "How are you?"

I already knew exactly how he was—bored. He had been forced into retirement the year prior when his factory closed and he was currently banging around the house like a guide dog whose owner had miraculously regained its sight. With his days free, he ran a copious amount of errands, flew through books, and started buying cheap DVDs from the mall. "That *In Living Color* is funny!" he once told me. I wasn't sure that a midfifties Indian immigrant really understood the nuances of Homey the Clown, but who was I to question my father's connection with the Wayan brothers? At least he had found ways to fill his time.

"Oh, fine," said Dad. He asked me briefly how New York was before saying, "You want to talk to your sister?"

"Um, sure," I responded. My sisters and I could easily make the best bomb-threat call-in team in the world. We rarely stayed on the phone with our parents for more than one minute, thus denying the FBI time to trace the call. "Damn it!" the Feds would say. "Damn, those Gills are the best!"

Navroop, who was visiting, came on the line. "Mom's not home," she stated.

"She can call me back later, then," I said. "How are you?"

Navroop was finishing up her master's in education and planning on going back to New Zealand, where she had lived for a year as an exchange student, after the New Year's holiday. On a whim, she had told our dad about it, but asked him to keep it to himself, as she was unsure of the plan. Sometimes he would slip up and say things like "Batteries are on sale. I'll go get some. You'll need them in New Zealand." Then he would say, "Oh, sorry, sorry, sorry," not wanting to lose Navroop's confidence and be thrown back into the ring of the uninformed. He would, of course, still go get the batteries.

"Can you swim yet?" she asked.

"Not yet," I said. "I don't know if I'm going to get it. It's just so scary."

I called home a few more times and talked to my mom about New York, but it was clear that she wasn't going to come. As successful as I was feeling about my journey of self-exploration, she was not willing to embark on an adventure herself. She worried about not being able to physically handle the long walks through the airport terminals and explore a city famous for walking. I stopped pressuring her, but I was disappointed. One of the most frustrating parts of going on a positive path is realizing that you can't drag other people along with you.

→ TWENTY-ONE ←

everybody loves *roti*

Part of my invitation to my mom to visit New York was precipitated by the memories of our time in India in the winter of 2008. When our flights were being booked, there was a possibility of flying through Europe, and she remarked, "Paris looks nice. Kuljit went there last time she went to India." For my mom to even express interest in a place meant she must have wanted to go there, but given that family always trumped opening new cultural horizons, our stopover was slated for the UK so my mom could visit her sister.

We traveled to India at the end of February, for a month-long visit. My mom and I were going with two of my dad's brothers, one of his sisters, and a gaggle of my cousins. In total, there were thirteen of us, one of the travelers being my twenty-six-year-old cousin who was going to get married. He lived in India before emigrating to Canada as a teenager and was now heading back to where his parents still lived for his wedding. He had only one month to rent a hall, send out the invitations, and most of all, to procure the bride.

This was still the norm in many parts of India. In bustling cities like Mumbai and Delhi, young people would meet prospective mates in nightclubs and coffee shops. They would date, sleep around, and play the field, looking for that elusive love marriage. Times had definitely changed, despite the desire of my parents to still believe that India is perpetually suspended in the culture of 1971. Whenever they would tell us we were losing touch with our culture, we would fire back that we would be happy to head down to the nearest bar and dance up against masses of sweaty Indian men, if they wanted us to act similarly to our counterparts back in the motherland.

But in rural Punjab, modernly arranged marriages were still the standard. Families would put out the word that a boy or girl was looking to get married and those with suitable matches would make themselves known. I use the word *modern* because instead of the parents being the decision makers, as would have been the case many decades ago, the couple now meets, goes on a series of supervised dates, and decides if they feel that they could be a suitable match.

My parents' marriage, of course, had been arranged in the traditional way. Their lives had always seemed so different from my sisters' and mine, and that trip reinforced those differences. Both of my parents were born and raised in rural towns in Punjab, India. "It was a carefree life," my dad would reminisce. "It was a lot less stressful there, life was very simple. Most of the village lived in mud houses."

Mud seemed to have a lot of uses in these early days. I vowed never to look at puddles with disdain again. Having grown up with brick and concrete housing me, it was difficult to imagine my father's family of eight living in a mud house, but my dad always looked back on their life as being idyllic.

"There was one radio in the village, given by the government," he said. "We would sit in the main *chonk* of the village and listen to the news. Not many people had watches. We would just go by the sun. I was eighteen years old when we got hydro for the first time. People were so excited."

My dad was a smarty-pants whose father struggled and came up with the money to put him through college, where he was the newspaper editor, class president, and overall best in show. He was the only one of six children who was ever sent to university, which was, back then, largely only for the affluent.

"Growing up, we were not rich and we were not poor," my dad would say. "We didn't have any money, but we didn't owe money to anybody either. Most of the village was like that."

My mother was a math champ, although the ability did not pass on to us. "Didn't you want to go to university?" we asked her once.

"Yes, I would have liked to go," she answered. "I liked school."

"What did you do for fun?" I asked her.

She paused to think it over. She rarely told us stories about her youth. It always seemed much more repressed than the fun we always heard about in our dad's household, where Bibi would chase them around the field with bars of soap.

"Marbles sometimes," she said. "Or we would jump rope. Mostly girls just helped around the house, though; we didn't have time to play."

Her life sounded more boring than watching TV all day.

"Didn't you EVER do anything fun?" I prodded.

"One time," she recounted fondly, "on our way to see a *gurdwara,* we went to see a Dharmendra film instead."

That was one of only two films she ever saw in the cinema growing up.

Their families lived in neighboring villages and knew each other well enough. And from those auspicious beginnings, a marriage was arranged. Most people's wedding photos are smiles and embraces. In theirs, my parents are standing at least five feet apart and my mother is wearing a shawl that covers her whole face, making her look like she bought her wedding outfit from the Emperor Palpatine bridal line. At the time, my father was already in Canada, where he took some courses at the University of Toronto before returning home to marry my mom. They then came back together, hoping for streets paved with gold and instead finding streets besieged with snow higher than sugarcane.

Like many immigrants, they gave up on careers in line with their educations and instead took whatever jobs were available and undesirable to natives of the country. In their case, it was in manual labor. They both worked in auto-industry-related factories. My mom would leave at 6 A.M. every day and my dad would rotate between working day and night shifts in a tire factory. His clothes always smelled like rubber when he came home. Living on an incredibly fixed income, they scrimped to sponsor their families to come over, and on my dad's side, all but one uncle made it through the immigration scrutiny. It was that uncle's son who was now getting married.

Going to India was my idea. The last time I had been there I was eighteen months old. My parents would sometimes tell me stories of how I pulled a baby goat around on a makeshift leash and cried because there was never enough meat on the bone when we ate chicken. But I have no memories of that six-month trip, just photos of a tanned little baby on her uncle's shoulders, straining to be seen over his turban.

With my cousin announcing his desire to get married, I knew it could be my last chance to go. My mom agreed to come so I wouldn't be alone, and at the end of February, we boarded a plane for the long voyage over. We weren't seated together for the first leg of the flight, so every hour or two I would feel a presence hovering above my seat and look up to see my mom, smiling and asking, "You are okay?"

I wasn't particularly a fan of flying, but flying an Indian airline made the experience all that much more memorable. Indians always seem to prefer to fly their native airlines, making it like a sit-down Mumbai bazaar in the plane. My dad had already warned me that since there would be a lot of elderly Indian men on the plane, I should "be careful because the old babas will pee all over the toilet seat."

On top of that, there were only three movies to view for the fifteen-hour flight, and all three were old Hindi films. Women shouted everywhere throughout the plane while an army of babies screamed at the top of their lungs.

After what felt like an unending journey, we neared our destination of Amritsar, the site of a famous Sikh holy shrine, the Golden Temple. It was two hours from my father's hometown, making it a much easier journey for our relatives than a ten-hour ride to Delhi.

Unfortunately, Delhi was where we were eventually going, whether we wanted to or not. Our flight was rerouted back there, due to fog. Two hours later, we landed in Delhi but were not allowed out of the plane for another five hours, when we were permitted into the terminal to sit idly for another three hours. I began to wonder if we would ever make it home when a group of male passengers, now inebriated and impatient, started screaming and dancing around the terminal, chanting derogatory yet hilarious-in-Hindi songs lampooning the airline.

By some strange meteorological coincidence, this embarrassing display of drunken protest somehow lifted the fog, because thirty minutes later we were back on our way, eight hours behind schedule.

When we arrived in Amritsar, my uncle drove us home in the pitch dark. The fog was still swirling menacingly, which made the shoddily paved drive home just a touch closer to lethal.

My poor mom's tiny body had been traumatized by the daylong expedition. The bumpy ride home tipped the scales of aggravation for her and caused her to vomit the whole ride to the village. Each time I turned around, she was clutching a plastic bag to her mouth, her face wincing with agony. When we finally arrived, we went straight to bed, thoroughly knackered from traveling halfway across the world.

In the morning I went outside to survey my new surroundings. The house was typical of those in the area, built around a paved courtyard. Ours was a bungalow. The main part of the house was occupied by my uncle and his wife and across the courtyard from them was my grandfather's room. He preferred to have his own area because the rest of the family routinely woke up at 5 A.M. for morning prayers.

A village in India is considered a large family compound. Marriages between people from the same village are frowned upon, as fellow villagers should only be viewed as an uncle or distant cousin. My grandfather's brother lived in the house next door to my dad's cousin, so most evenings the two elders would stand at the foot of our dirt road, talking politics and village affairs.

Due partially to cost and mostly to the fact that the electricity blows out a minimum of four times a day, air-conditioning was not a standard fixture. Instead, a series of large windows and screened doors let the breezes travel through the whole length of the house. Spiraling stairs led to the roof deck, which allowed a view of the whole village, green pastures dotted with houses, growing more gargantuan with each passing year.

It was quiet in the village. Noisewise, it was actually quite loud, with the sound of bus horns blaring and parrots squawking constantly. But actionwise, it was sleepy living at its best and worst. We went to sleep when the sky got dark and awoke at ungodly hours when the sun first emerged. Alarm clocks were never necessary. The majority of the time was spent sitting around the house, visiting with nearby relatives, or dropping by to see relatives I had never met in neighboring villages.

They would smile and nod and offer us the chai to which they were all addicted, then smile again, perplexed, when I said that I didn't drink it.

Motioning toward me, they would ask my mom, "How old is the goodie?"

Twenty-nine was not the answer they expected to hear. "Goodie" was a term of endearment used for a young girl and I was slowly rotting in the marriage basket, likely four years overripe and now fairly classifiable as a "baddie."

I have to admit that people were a lot more gracious about my single status than I expected. I had seriously considered whether or not it was wise to even go, because it was an open invitation to be judged on being unmarried by relatives whose names I didn't even know.

My cousin, though he had spent the past decade in Canada and dated during that time, felt that the traditional method of marriage was best for him. In fact, not one of my marriage-age cousins on either side has made a love marriage. Whether they lived in the UK or Canada, they have all thus far chosen to marry according to tradition. Most married other foreign born Indians, but a few male cousins also chose to travel to India to look for a bride. This is most commonly done by men, as India is full of young, beautiful women who can overlook a few flaws in their mate in order to gain citizenship in another country. Like most cultures, Indians also put emphasis on what the man does for a living, with little interest in whether or not the woman is employed at all.

That wedding would be one of three that we would attend during our month in India. The first of the nuptials was between two nineteen-year-olds from the UK. After learning my age, the bride nudged her friend and said, "She's twenty-nine!" to her friends, who looked over with expressions of disbelief that my tiny face and childlike balloon hair would be that aged, and pity that I was still unmarried. I was aware, even in that moment, that if we were standing in a city in North America, instead of on a dirt road in India, it would be me and my friends who would have expressions of horror at the thought of being married one year after graduating high school.

Indians are obsessed with marriage. This has three possible reasons:

1. Marriage really is the bee's knees.
2. Wedding-buffet Samosas are laced with cocaine, leaving the guests desperately anticipating the next nuptials.
3. They are so miserable in their own marriages that they want to pull you down with them.

I give my parents credit for not pressuring their kids to marry.

Although people would make snide remarks about my parents'—or at least my father's—liberal attitude, they in turn were kind enough to not parlay such criticism into a massive guilt trip on us for being single. Even after our cousins, some younger than us, started down the marriage path.

To test the waters, we would often ask our parents what they thought of our marrying a man who was not Indian. My dad, educated and so well read that his library contained everything from Kahlil Gibran to the poetry of Jewel (I swear it was on sale), had no issue with it.

"Marry whom you want," he would say. "Maybe people will talk about you, but even if you marry an Indian, they will talk about you. They will always find a reason to talk about you."

This was true, and hearing it took a certain amount of weight off my shoulders.

My mom would then load the weight back. She is a lot more traditional than my dad. Where Christians ask themselves, "What would Jesus do?" Indians ask themselves, "What will people say?" Both questions offer difficult standards to live up to, but only one offered the promise of salvation.

"I don't know," she would answer.

"So if we married someone white and had a baby, you wouldn't love it?" we prodded.

"Well, I guess I would have to," she said with a cringe that betrayed her real thoughts.

Over the years you would think that my mom would have adopted the beggars-can't-be-choosers mentality toward marriage. Gurpreet and I were over thirty and still nowhere close to donning wedding saris, but still my mom was holding out for those perfect Indian husbands. They would need to be of the right religion, caste, professional and educational background, and for some reason, be interested in brides near their expiration dates instead of nubile twenty-one-year-olds who would much rather whip up a perfect pork vindaloo than order sushi.

This might be surprising to hear but my feelings toward marriage definitely leaned more to Indian values than North American ones. I think marriage is forever. Indian marriages don't stop when a person becomes fat. They don't end because someone wants to "find themselves" or is getting flirty compliments from the new assistant at work.

Indian marriages don't carry the delusion of being madly in love forever, or promise everlasting fire in the bedroom. They are based on teamwork, compromise, and the shared understanding that whatever the issue, the couple had to weather the storm together.

In fairness, it is also true that belief in the till-death-do-us view of marriage can trap people in terrible marriages. And in most cases it is the woman who is stuck. In a society that is still patriarchal, the men call the shots and women are forced to suffer the consequences.

I recall hearing, when I was a young girl, of female family acquaintances who were in abusive or unhealthy relationships. But even at that young age, I knew that nobody was going to be stepping in to do anything about it. It was also at this time that I realized that I would likely never marry another Indian. Almost every one of my married cousins is married to another Indian, and from the outside, the unions all look to be happy ones. Marriage conventions have advanced somewhat, and the prospective bride and groom now take time to get to know each other through coffee-shop dates, phone conversations, or visits.

But despite the modernization of the arrangement, I always felt that at some point, in a way so slight that it annoyed me or so large that it drove me to depression, the traditional gender roles would emerge and I would find myself accused of "not respecting his mother enough" or not making chai that was strong enough for his brother's palate.

Although we were attending three weddings of people younger than I was, my mom didn't bring the subject of marriage up with me during the trip, which I greatly appreciated. She did, however, treat me like I was ten.

I hadn't spent more than three consecutive days with my mom for a number of years and now I was sharing a bed with her for a month and having to run my plans by her before I acted on them.

"Okay, I'm going into town," I announced one day, grabbing my purse. One of my cousins and I would sometimes take the motorized rickshaw bus into town and wander around, eat Samosas, then return home.

This particular time, I was facing resistance.

"No, you're not," my mom said. "We have to go visit people today and you have to come."

"Why do I have to?!" I yelled. "They don't care about seeing me. I've never even met them. Just go yourself."

In the end, I had to go, hair plastered down like a five-year-old schoolgirl, nodding politely along to the conversation and slowly sipping my Fanta. If my mom was going to revert back to being the mother of a first grader, I was going to act like that first grader.

"I'm so bored here," I said. "Why can't we travel and see some of India? Are we going to sit in the village forever?"

"You know," my mom said, "that's what people do. We come here to see people, not tour around. I have never seen the Taj Mahal."

"Then let's go," I said. "Let's finally see it."

She gave in, and with our uncle's family, we hired a driver and drove from Punjab through to India's midsection to see the famous sights.

The Taj Mahal was beautiful and eerie all at once, the most elaborate tomb and declaration of love one would ever see.

"What do you think?" I said.

"It's very nice," my mom responded. "People are supposed to come here on their honeymoons." I didn't know if that was genuine Indian tradition or a dig at me, but I let it slide.

The Pink City of Jaipur was bustling and fascinating. The Red Fort was magnificent and Fatehpur Sikri was an incredible voyage back to the sixteenth-century home of the Mughal empire. My mom was a trooper during the tours, a lot of which involved excessive amounts of stairs and walking, but sometimes she was forced to sit out. Still, she had finally seen some of the highlights of her native country, more than thirty years after leaving it.

While my mom did get to finally see the Taj Mahal, she wasn't going to get to see the Statue of Liberty. It was likely for the best, as walking would have probably been an issue in a city the size of New York. But I didn't want to give up on sharing the experience I was having with my family, in some way. The year had been a great one for me thus far. I had time for truly unabashed self-reflection and focus, a rare opportunity unless you have a trust fund or are on sabbatical at a Buddhist monastery. I wanted to do something for my family as well. We had all lived lives of set-aside dreams and less than happy memories, from my parents right down to my little brother. None of us had ever seen Disney World. In fact, in all my years, we had never even gone on a family vacation together. Never once had we sat on a plane together. Never once had we sat down to a meal in a restaurant together. It had never been economically or logistically possible and my parents never deemed these things anywhere close to a priority.

But now that my siblings and I were adults, my parents no longer ran our family and I decided that if I was going to Disney World, I would do it as our long-overdue family vacation. I wanted to say that it would be better late than never, but visions in my mind of the fighting, nagging, negativity, and pettiness to come crossed my mind. Still, with so few memories of note from our childhood, why not throw one bittersweet one in from the present? With that plan in place, I sent a note to the PR team at Disney World through their online portal. Now living an unstable wannabe writer's life, I didn't have the means to pay for a family of seven's holiday. But sometimes you have to get crafty to make your dreams come true.

→ TWENTY-TWO ←

come and knock on my door

One of the best things about New York is that someone is always in town. The roaches decided to find a new home, leaving me space for visitors. Jen and Jaclyn came to visit on a sunny weekend in early October. More for my sake than theirs, Jaclyn's husband and Jen's mom bought them tickets to visit as gifts. I could tell that they had arrived when I heard Jen's voice project from the lobby, asking one of my neighbors, "Isn't there an elevator?!"

I flung the door open and skipped down the stairs, grabbing their smaller bags so they could lug their giant suitcases to the apartment.

"You're just here for the weekend, right?" I said, eyeing the bursting bags.

"They aren't full," Jaclyn said. "But they sure will be when we leave!"

She wasn't kidding. That night we met up with Mel and Madeleine for a gastronomic overload and the next day consisted of a shopping marathon. Shopping is not my ideal pastime, especially because my New York sabbatical seemed to be costing me a tenner each and every New York minute, but I obliged my friends because amazing bargain clothes souvenirs are a must for returning home from New York.

Shopping actually ended up being a perfect plan of action because the day was a steady downpour of rain. It was not a day made for sauntering through the city with an ice-cream cone in hand. Instead, I sprinted between stores while the out-of-towners tried on every pair of shoes and all the cute blouses available in the city. Although the day followed a typical tourists-shopping-madly schedule, strangely it made me feel more at home. I had two more familiar faces in the midst and was easily navigating them around the town that I was getting the hang of. It had taken me a month but I was finally feeling at home.

When they left the next day, their suitcases were nearly splitting at the seams and I was sad to see them go.

"See you in a month," I said as their car pulled up to the curb.

"I'll pick you up at the airport," Jaclyn offered.

"Thanks," I said. "If I don't make it home, I'm living in a penthouse with a handsome heir of some kind and will need you to send my winter coat."

"We'll await word," Jen joked.

. . .

On Monday afternoon, my phone blinked to alert me of a message. It was Freddie. "Hey, Rupinder," he said. "I have some bad news."

This sounded ominous. I wondered if a security camera had caught me helping myself to more than my fair share of lotion in the women's locker room.

"I don't know if I can teach you anymore," Freddie said. "I just got another job, so am not free on Wednesdays anymore. Maybe we could do evenings if you still want to work with me. We can discuss it on Wednesday."

I showed up early for my third lesson. A lane at the end of the pool was reserved for something labeled as "water walking." A quick survey of the lane revealed this to be anything from floating on your back with a pool noodle immodestly jutting out between your legs to standing and talking to your poker buddies by the ladder while wearing matching Speedos. The mean age for lane entry appeared to be seventy.

I changed and headed out to the pool area, contemplating a water walk. Freddie waved hello when he spied me swathed in towels and motioned toward our usual lane. "Why don't you jump in and start practicing your breathing," he suggested. Shedding the towels, I immersed myself in the water. I stood at the side of the wall, counted, and plunged my head in the water for as long as I could. After a few minutes, Freddie came over.

"Congratulations on the job," I said.

We spent a few minutes revisiting the basics before he challenged me to float, then throw my arms and legs into the mix. Backing up to the wall, I took a deep breath, kicked off with my feet, and coasted just beneath the surface. After a few seconds I started moving my legs and pulling myself with my arms. When the oxygen supplies were beginning to deplete, I surfaced to a hero's welcome.

"Great job!" Freddie smiled. "Have you been practicing?"

"Actually no," I admitted. "I think I'm just a little less freaked out," I said.

"Works for me." He laughed. "How do you feel about going into the deep end?"

"Errr . . ." I stammered, confidence waning by the second. "Do you think I'm ready?"

"Why not?" he asked.

I could think of a million reasons why not, the top ten including my watery death and the top hundred including various versions of a scenario in which I pull ten unsuspecting swimmers down with me and/or soil myself in the pool. But I knew that whether I wanted to or not, I was going to have to venture into the deep end. Otherwise, I would pretty much be limited to water walking forever.

"Jump in," Freddie coaxed as I stood frozen on the deck.

"Right now?" I asked.

"Whenever you're ready," Freddie said.

"Hmm . . . okay, what year is it now?" I joked.

"Just take your time," he said.

I breathed in first shallowly, then deeply, then took a series of shallow breaths, then longer yoga breaths. I looked at the water rippling and wondered if there could be any possible riptides lurking beneath.

"Just jump," Freddie said.

Readying myself another few seconds, I closed my eyes and launched myself into the water. When I hit the surface, I opened my eyes and saw myself sinking lower and lower toward the lines at the bottom of the pool. I prayed it wasn't like the movie *Abyss,* where the seafloor opened to show that it extended another thousand or so feet downward.

I soon bounced back from the bottom and reached desperately for the side of the wall once oxygen refilled my lungs.

"You did it!" Freddie exclaimed from his safe perch on the deck.

I had penetrated deep water! This was a feat for me. And although I immediately wanted to get right back out of it, I put my faith in Freddie.

The rest of the session was occupied by my valiant and fairly unsuccessful attempts at treading water. This was really the difficult part of swimming for me. I didn't mind swimming underwater; it was the attempt to remain buoyant at the surface that was the problem for me. This is where the flailing and panic would set in.

"Just be calm," Freddie said. "I'm right here if you need me."

When I was done with the lesson, I felt no more comfortable with the deep end just because I had experienced it. Just because a claustrophobic lives through one elevator ride doesn't mean she's ready to jam herself into another one when the opportunity arises. But unfortunately, only repeated exposure would dull my terror, so I would have to jump back in next time and the time after that, until doing so no longer occupied my thoughts the hours prior to each scheduled swimming experience.

At least I had the sauna to look forward to afterward.

TWENTY-THREE

i dream of tv

The next weekend, my friend Hannah came to visit. She was always great fun, and as an added bonus, her personality consisted of guidance counselor and cheerleader all in one and that meant some good conversations about life and goals. So far, New York and time off work had failed to completely defog my head, so advice from an objective party was going to be beneficial. She and a friend had driven down from Toronto for five days with a full agenda of concerts, meetings, and social affairs.

An old colleague of Hannah's had moved to New York to work on *Late Night with Jimmy Fallon* and gave Hannah and her friends tickets to attend a taping. When she extended the invitation my way, I jumped at the chance. Growing up, my sisters and I created a summer routine of staying up to watch every late show and then sleeping until approximately nine hours after whatever time we ultimately called it a night.

The show was great, but the best part was afterward, when we assembled in the lobby to be taken on a behind-the-scenes tour.

"This is Rupinder," Hannah introduced me to our guide, Tim. "She's a writer, too."

I shot her a look of extreme embarrassment, as I didn't want to stand in the middle of 30 Rockefeller Plaza detailing my blog posts about the best back-to-school binders.

"Oh, cool," said Tim.

He took us back to a studio to show us the behind-the-scenes action, then took us down a floor to the studio where *Saturday Night Live* was shot.

"This is the set," he said, taking us around the set of one of the shows I had watched every weekend of my youth. The cast was in their dress rehearsal, so we all strained to see if we could catch any of the action just as the doors started closing.

"Was that Bono?" I asked Hannah excitedly.

"It *did* look like him," she said.

As I walked through the sets and sniffed at the craft services table, I became aware of something that I had kept so deep inside of myself forever: I wanted to do this, too.

Okay, I admit it: EVERYONE wants to work in show business. I fully acknowledge this fact. Every kid from Missouri on the bus to Hollywood and every waiter, waitress, housewife, and pool boy in the greater Los Angeles area wants it. It was likely one of the dumbest career paths I could ever choose.

My friend Ilana had recently moved from television production to a job at a talent agency. "I remember seeing a guy I recognized at our Christmas party," Ilana said when I'd spoken with her recently. "I knew I had worked with him but I couldn't place him. I asked my boss who he was and she told me that it was one of our screenwriters. It was then that I recognized him as one of the set decorators from the show I worked on last year."

Everybody has a streak of the artistic in them. And for every hustling writer and starstruck wannabe actor in Hollywood, there are a hundred more people sitting at home with dreams of it but no plan of pursuit. I understood that, but by this point I had crazy notions about anything being possible.

Besides my early interest in television, I had Malcolm Gladwell's assessment of genius on my side. In his book *Outliers,* Gladwell outlines the path to success by telling the tales of geniuses like Bill Gates and physicist J. Robert Oppenheimer. Gladwell hypothesizes that outliers are individuals who have the perfect combination of opportunity, timing, and experience to become leaders in their respective fields.

Based on this equation, this made me predestined to be a TV genius. Because I didn't have the opportunity to go out, I had the opportunity to watch television for an inhuman number of hours. My timing was perfect because television was evolving rapidly every year. And experience? This is where I really shone.

In my lifetime, I have easily put in twenty thousand hours watching TV. If that seems an exaggeration, this chart of my average TV schedule will illustrate:

Summer vacation ages seven to fourteen:
10 A.M.: *Welcome Back, Kotter*
11 A.M.: *Three's Company*
12 P.M.: Lunch—two hot dogs or a pizza pita, based on availability
1 P.M.: *Days of our Lives*
2 P.M.: *One Life to Live*
3 P.M.: *General Hospital*
4 P.M.: *Golden Girls*
5 P.M.: *Empty Nest*
6 P.M.: *Nurses*

This was strictly my daytime viewing. My sisters and I would likely log another hour or two at night, of *Dallas, Perfect Strangers, The A-Team,* or *Magnum, P.I.* Gurpreet and I once cried at the dentist's office because we were missing a new episode of *The A-Team* that was airing that night. This was still nowhere near as devastating as when we heard that David Hasselhoff and the KITT car from *Knight Rider* were coming to our neighborhood Toys "R" Us store. We were driving to visit our cousins north of Toronto, so would pass the store on our drive.

"Please!" we screamed to our dad as we spied the store approaching on the side of the highway. "Please, we'll be fast! . . . It's our favorite show! The car's here!"

My dad was not budging. "We don't have time."

"Please, please, please, please," we screamed.

"Who cares about DAZZLE HASSELHOFF?" he said as he drove right past the store.

We did. We cared about the man he thought was named

Dazzle. He entertained us every Monday night and we were willing to wait in a line for five hours for the chance to thank him for it.

If you multiplied my daily viewing by approximately eighty days of summer, the tally was 800 hours just in three months. In those seven summers alone, the grand total was a whopping 4,800 hours. Even this seemed a conservative estimate, as we went through a phase of a few years when we were heavily into tennis viewing. Adding my school-year viewing to that, in the fifteen years that followed, I could have easily doubled the estimated number. And Gladwell thought that Bill Gates was dedicated.

My time in New York was drawing to a close and I made a mental note to set up some meetings with people in television when I returned home. After five years in the industry, I had enough of a network to sit down with people and solicit some much-needed advice.

In my last few weeks in New York, I still had a lot to accomplish. After meeting Natasha and thinking harder about her attitude toward her background vs. mine, I realized I really needed to rediscover my culture on my own terms.

I had been jaded about my culture for too long. When I was a kid, if someone made a T-shirt that said "My Parents Left India and All I Got Was Nagged Every Day," I would have bought a dozen. But my general bitterness levels were decreasing over the current year, and with that blossomed a genuine interest in all things Indian.

I loved the films of Mira Nair, Deepa Mehta, and Satyajit

Ray. They helped me gain a deeper understanding of the culture I knew too little of, and opened my eyes to the beauty and complexity of India. I loved great stories about India starring people who looked like me, but I was less enthralled with the modern-day films out of Bollywood. When I was younger I would sing songs from the classic films starring icons like Amitabh Bachchan and Shashi Kapoor, but the contemporary films were just way too long for my impatience, so I was very behind on my Bollywood knowledge.

I loved Indian food but wasn't proficient at making it, and my siblings' and my conversations with our parents would consist of my parents speaking to us in Punjabi while we answered back in English. My Punjabi language skills had largely fallen away since my dad tried to teach Gurpreet and me how to read and write it twenty years ago.

We would cringe when we heard him call us for our lessons, mostly because we were caught up in one of our favorite soaps. But he would summon us up to the family room and we would skulk there, with our matching binders and copies of his text of choice, *Punjabi Made Easy*.

His exaggerated pronunciation of each word was meant to help us master the phonetics, but what it actually did was make us break into fits of giggles.

"Ittttttttt-aaaaa," he would say, pointing to a picture of a brick.

"Haaaaa-theeeeee," he enunciated to the photo of the elephant.

"Stop laughing!" he would yell, but we couldn't comply. In the end he would give up, assign us homework, and give us a reprieve until the next lesson.

By the time Navroop and Navjit reached the age Gurpreet and I had been at the time of the language lessons, a real Punjabi school existed, set up by members of our local *gurdwara*. They met in a nearby hockey arena and worked their way through the Punjabi alphabet with other local Punjabi kids. Although Gurpreet and I became proficient enough to be called up to display our skills to guests, I had now largely forgotten how to read and write the language. Even my speaking skills were becoming more and more rudimentary with lack of practice.

Riding the L train one night, I saw an ad for a night called "Basement Bhangra" in a magazine, and realized that it was time to finally have that Indian night I had planned. I roped Madeleine and Melissa into accompanying me. Apparently it was *the* Punjabi party night in New York City, so it sounded like a perfect place for our evening.

The dance party was held in a Latino dance club, in order to really drive home the multicultural flavor of New York. As we sat in the dining area watching the crowd fill the dance floor, I was surprised that most of the partygoers were anything but Indian. Just when I thought that I had been mistaken about this being the Indian hot spot, three separate posses of Indians entered the club.

"Okay, everybody," a petite Indian girl shouted from the stage. "Come on down to the dance floor and let's all learn how to Bhangra!"

This would have mortified me as a kid. When my sisters and I were dragged to weddings of people we barely knew, we never felt comfortable dancing and thus would hide out anxiously for hours so nobody would drag us up to the dance floor. We didn't know how to dance and didn't want to uncomfortably clap and dance in a circle, just to have some bitchy auntie say, "My, you really looked funny up there," to us later. We were generally so self-conscious about our very beings that we knew how to shelter ourselves from attention and its related criticism. While cousins and family friends showed off their best Madhuri Dixit–style dance moves, we would stuff ourselves at the buffet and say, "Sure, sure, after we eat," or pretend we were in deep conversations with a toddler to avoid being pulled up by an overzealous auntie.

But when I was in India, I grew tired of sitting on the sidelines and just decided to get up and dance, regardless of the fact that I had not heard most of the songs before and had no idea what I was doing. It was a lot easier and more enjoyable than hiding out at the buffet during three different weddings and all their festivities.

Now, in New York, not only was I going to dance, I had paid twenty dollars and waited in line for the pleasure. I felt like a party girl in Mumbai. As the crowd cheered, the three of us ran down to the dance floor to get our groove on. After teaching us how to properly wind our hips and move our arms, the instructor invited people up to the stage to showcase their new moves.

Melissa waved her hand and screamed to be invited. Ignoring the backpack she was toting, she ran onstage and linked ankles with the man beside her, hopping around with her arms hoisted in the air. She was hooked. After she'd been dancing for five minutes, they had to ask her twice to leave.

After the lesson, people were huddled in small groups on the dance floor for further lessons from fellow dancers. Four middle-aged European women were gathered around one older Indian gentleman who was coaching them as they swayed their hips.

"More arms," he suggested, throwing his arms up to the heavens, "like you're offering something to the sky."

On the other side of the room, a crowd was gathered around two turbaned men who were putting on an impressive show of Bhangra prowess. Bhangra really is a man's dance. Women have fun doing it, but at weddings, it is the men who hoist one another onto their shoulders and dance around wildly, doing everything from Ra-Ra-Rasputin kicks to impromptu coordinated routines while singing Bollywood tunes at the top of their lungs.

The dance floor was now packed and sweat was rolling down our faces. Melissa and I tried several unsuccessful ankle links and we all danced around to Bollywood beats, laughing at the girls who were trying to make it sexy by doing belly-dancing moves instead.

As the crowd whooped and hollered, we kept dancing and the dance floor became more and more crowded.

"Should we get going?" Madeleine said.

"Ya, it's late," we agreed, and kept on dancing.

Half an hour later, I was nearly exhausted. "Okay, we should go," I said.

"Absolutely," they said, and still continued to dance.

We just couldn't tear ourselves away. Finally, at two in the morning, we had to call it a night. As a grand finale to our evening, we danced out of the bar in a line, like a Bhangra *Soul Train*.

"That was SO much fun!" Melissa said when we got outside. It was busy inside, but nothing compared to outside, where a line of people was snaking down the street.

"We have to do that again," Madeleine said.

"Definitely," I agreed.

Had my father never left India, would this be my life? I wondered. Would I be dancing every Saturday night to Bhangra music at my local disco? I knew that in actuality, if my father had never left, we would still be farmers in Punjab and I would never have had the chance to do anything—including attend university or see New York. I would likely already have been married with young children like all of my cousins in India. My marriage would have been arranged, and my days would consist of tending a growing household. In my lifetime, I would likely never leave India or be aware of the world outside of it. I may have unfulfilled desires from my youth, but overall, I was aware that I was pretty damn lucky.

→ TWENTY-FOUR ←

give my regards to broadway

My last week in New York felt more bittersweet than I had anticipated. I missed people at home, I missed cable, and I missed my stuff—my books, my paintings, my souvenirs from trips, things that expressed my personality. But I wanted to stay. More than anything, I wanted to be able to stay. I was now acclimatized to the city. I could offer people directions with confidence and I loved nothing more than a full afternoon spent reading in Central Park. As the fall sun shone its face on me, I would flip through the pages of everyone from Camus and Woody Allen to Judy Blume and feel instantly at home in my adopted city.

The thing that really attracted me to the city was the unabashed positivity of everyone I met. Saying "I'd love to write for television" was met with a chorus of "Great idea!"

and "Yes, you definitely should do that." Discussing my year of self-improvement and my last two months of unemployment were always met with encouragement. New York was where people came to make their dreams come true and there was encouragement for a wide variety of dreams.

I felt as if I had left my job ten years ago. Being in a different city, so far removed from my previous job and life, made that past slip further and further away. It's not that I thought I would sit in the park reading forever. I knew I needed to work again. In fact, I looked forward to working again. I longed for the very same hyperscheduling and time constraints I had formerly bemoaned. But for the time being, I was relishing my new reality. It had taken me a while to settle into it and now it felt like a warm cocoon from which I didn't want to emerge.

I spent my last week being a tourist and wrapping up loose ends. MoMA had a special members-only viewing of portions of Monet's *Water Lilies* series. Robert Evans tells a great story in *The Kid Stays in the Picture* about being offered the chance to buy a painting. He gazes upon it, falls instantly under its spell, and then doesn't end up buying it. It was one of the *Water Lilies.* When I ascended the escalator and entered the gallery, there were only four other people in the room, including an old Indian couple. The woman wore a maroon sari and a pair of running shoes and the man ushered her around slowly with his hand on her elbow. I could never imagine my parents making plans to gaze upon a famous piece of art. It was a decadent use of time when there were so many things to be done. Looking at the vast expanses of canvas, I was pulled in.

I took a seat on the bench, bobbing my head from one painting to the next, staring at the swirls of color, the beautiful muted tones, and the lyrical beauty of natural life in Giverny. I had a list of errands to complete in my pocket, but having lived my whole life as a type A personality with so many demands placed on me by myself, I felt compelled to stay seated.

I had only one last task to attack before heading home. I really wanted to drive in Manhattan. I was ready to careen through the crowded streets, honking and flailing my arms at my fellow drivers, calling out "Moron!" or "Jackass!" In turn, I would offer a blind eye and ear to the various honks and raised middle fingers on every side of me. This was the delicate dance known as driving in a big city.

On what must have been the rainiest day since Noah's maiden voyage, I ran over from Union Square to the driving school on Twenty-third Street. By the time I arrived at the office, I was drenched from the waist down, a result of my umbrella's annoying practical joke of blowing itself inside out. "Have a seat," the receptionist instructed. "We'll call your instructor." A minute later my cell phone rang and displayed an unknown number. "Rupinder?" the voice asked. "It's Jin, your instructor. I'm parked on Twenty-second and Park. It's impossible to find parking in front of the office."

How quintessentially New York: a driving school that couldn't even find parking in front of its own building. I ran back down the street and found Jin sitting in a maroon Toyota. I jumped into the passenger seat and introduced myself, and he said, "Maybe you should try it from over here." I jumped back out and we played musical chairs while trying to dodge the rain.

"I haven't driven a lot," I warned him. "And I have never driven here. I'm from Canada."

"Canada," he said, smiling. "Quebec City is so beautiful. Okay, start driving."

And with that, I put on my turn signal, checked my mirrors, and pulled out onto Twenty-third Street.

I sure hope Jin knew what he was doing, because I couldn't say the same for myself. I was used to parallel parking in empty parking lots and now I was cruising up Park Avenue and checking my mirror for frail socialites who might be in my blind spot.

"Okay, turn left," Jin instructed after a few blocks. Checking every mirror possible, I inched into the intersection and turned onto Third Avenue, then back onto a quiet side street where I sat behind an idling mattress delivery truck for two minutes before turning to Jin and asking, "May I?"

He nodded and I laid on the horn until the truck inched forward.

"You're like a native New Yorker!" Jin laughed.

Driving in Manhattan was actually easier than I thought it would be. This was mostly due to the fact that your car barely moves an inch every minute. We drove around and around the West Village, then back to the East Village. I had never seen Union Square from inside a car before and I took the opportunity to honk and motion at all the jaywalking teenagers that I was powerless to properly judge when I was a pedestrian myself.

"Thank you so much," I said to Jin when I turned back onto Twenty-third Street to end the lesson. "How am I as a driver?"

"You're very good," he said. "Definitely above average."

Above average. I was more than pleased with that.

My last swimming lesson was scheduled for the day before I was leaving. As Freddie was busy at his other job during the days now, we were meeting in the evening. I awoke that morning with a monster cold that could not be quelled by any type of cold remedy. It seemed that the whole town had it, as Melissa, Ken, and Madeleine were also ill.

I spent the day packing up my home for the past few months and tying up loose ends. That evening I ran out into the pouring rain to meet Freddie for the last time. Friday night was very obviously the family swim night at the pool. It was crammed with kids of all ages splashing about.

"Last lesson!" Freddie said.

I had progressed well on the previous lesson. I jumped into the deep end whenever Freddie commanded, I stayed under the water for as long as I could stand, and I counted out strokes in my mind to capture the proper rhythm of swimming. When water went up my nose, I jumped back in and tried it again. With my time in New York drawing to a close, I wanted to feel as if I had achieved as much as possible. Whether or not I jumped into the deep end was completely within my control. So I had to make it happen.

On this fifth and last lesson, my cold was making it difficult to catch a proper breath or have the energy to attempt a lap. Another hindrance was a little girl who may have been a mermaid, swimming in the same lane as me.

"Zoey," her mother called out. "Watch the lady!"

Yes, Zoey. Please watch the lady. The second I would extend an arm for a stroke, it would hit Zoey. When I put my head under the water, there was Zoey coming right at me to retrieve a toy from the bottom of the pool. When I floated on my back, Zoey splashed a downpour of water onto my face.

"How do you feel about jumping into the deep end?" Freddie asked.

"Not very good at all," I said. No doubt Zoey would be lurking there as well.

I gave up and jumped in. Freddie forced me to tread water and continue attempting laps until we both agreed that the pool had become a danger zone. Kids were now dominating my lane, splashing around with their parents or chasing each other with flutter boards.

We decided to wrap it up because there was no more space, and because I was one minute from trying to wipe my nose with a pool noodle.

"Thank you so much for everything," I said to Freddie. "I promise I'll keep going. When I can swim three laps, I'll call you and let you know."

"Good luck with everything," Freddie said as we shook hands in the water.

I went to enjoy one last sauna, then called Melissa and Ken to arrange a rendezvous. We all met on the corner and took the bus over to Madeleine's. I was on my way to my NYC good-bye party.

"I can't believe you're already leaving," Ken said.

"Neither can I," I said.

Melissa and Ken gave me a lovely going-away gift: a writing book with a photograph of the L train on the cover.

"I know you'll miss riding that every day," Melissa said.

I would. I would miss that sharp turn between Bedford and First Avenue stops that usually sent me flying, once into the lap of a man nearby. I would miss the excitement of heading into the city and getting off on the Upper West Side to wander through the park or downtown for an impromptu dinner. But going home was the best step for me. I needed to get everything in place for a chance to return to NYC once again, and not just as a traveler.

Until then, I had a lot of work to do. The foray into television was going poorly. In Canada, if you looked up talent agencies, you could eventually find your way to an agent's name. No matter how sharp my Googling skills had become, I could not find the names of agents at any of the large U.S. talent agencies. There were more than enough sites that generously offered me that information, along with a star map, for the tidy sum of $49.99, but I was wary of their claim that I was just one click away from "lunch with Spielburg [*sic*] and Scorsese."

I knew that if I wanted to finish off my list of goals, I was going to have to ask for some help. On the last episode of *Murphy Brown* I had watched, Murphy advised Corky to reach for that brass ring and never take her eye off the prize. The advice of a fictitious television journalist was good enough for me.

One prize fell into my lap on my last day in New York. I was sitting in a coffee shop down the street from my building when my phone rang to display a Canadian number. "Is this Rupinder?" a happy voice inquired on the other end.

"Hi, this is Angela from Walt Disney World Canada."

Wow, I had only written last week. They really did answer those wishes upon stars.

"I got your request," Angela said, "and I would love to help you out if I can."

Angela and I chatted for a bit.

"So nobody in your family has ever been?" she said.

"No," I said. I offered my rehearsed impassioned plea, to which she could fully relate, having grown up as a child of immigrants herself.

"I completely understand," she said. "My parents are Greek."

"I can give you guys some passes to go," she said. "Just let me know when you're going and who's going with you. I think you'll really like it."

"That's so generous of you," I said. "I can't say thank you enough!"

Another life lesson learned: it never ever hurts to ask.

part three

→ TWENTY-FIVE ←

let's make a *daal*

Back in Toronto, I was on a mission. I was pleased with what I had accomplished during the year. But now that I had a goal in mind for my life, not just for the year, I had a lot of work to do.

"So when do you have to go back to work?" my parents asked me when I went to visit them in mid-November.

"Oh, not for a while," I replied, anticipating the question.

They nodded and my mom went back to watching *Desperate Housewives.* After three decades in North America, she and my father had at last become fans of television.

"Did you see *Becker*?" my mom would ask my dad. He would admit that he had and they would laugh about a joke they both loved in a sitcom that had been canceled at least three years prior.

My mom was making my favorite chicken-and-rice dish. Growing up, I would hide out in the basement when she made it so I wouldn't have to help in the hours-long process, come upstairs to eat, and then run back down. This time I wanted to learn to make it myself. She pulled out canisters of spices and jars of fresh ginger and garlic, and started piling up all the ingredients on the counter. Indian food has so many deliciously complex flavors because it's deliciously complex to make.

"Now you put the ginger into the food processor," my mom explained in Punjabi as I furiously tried to write the instructions down.

"How much?" I asked in English.

"Now you have to add the tomatoes and the garlic and the masala," my mom continued. I had to turn over the piece of paper to continue writing. I measured out the rice and checked all the salt levels, and one hour later, the meal was made.

As was customary, I was the one who tested the chicken for salt and flavor, then I was the one who ate first, helping myself to the most tender of the breasts and ladling broth all over the rice. After adding a layer of yogurt on top, I created a messy paste and consumed plate after plate.

Unfortunately I didn't fare as well when I attempted to make the dish myself the next week. I had to improvise, as I did not have all of the necessary fresh ingredients. My rice came out sticky and the chicken mildly bland, but I was going to keep at it until I had the recipe down, then I would go back to my mom for another one.

Not having seen some of my friends for months, I figured

this was the perfect time to take another crack at a sleepover. Jen, Jaclyn, and Maggie came over on a Friday night. I was prepared with copies of *The Lost Boys* and the original *Fame*, as well as bags of chips and pints of ice cream. We had decided to order dinner out, but we all knew it would not be a large pepperoni pizza. Maggie was a vegetarian who ate only low-fat food. Jen didn't eat red meat and Jaclyn didn't eat fast food.

"Um . . . I'll get the tofu bowl," I said when Jaclyn called to take my dinner order. If I was going to ask three grown women to come over for a sleepover in my downtown apartment, I had to concede on some issues. Besides, I loved the tofu bowl.

Jen had brought a *Sweet Valley High* puzzle over and we discussed what sleepover-related activities to conquer.

"We could egg a house!" Jen said.

We all ruled that out because we were too old to risk being arrested and I only had six organic free-range eggs in the fridge. We ruled out summoning Bloody Mary in the washroom because that's the kind of sleepover activity that girls did after about three bottles of smuggled-from-home alcohol.

We were old enough to buy our own alcohol but of an age when the bottle of wine remained half full halfway through the night.

We did, however, decide to do drugs. Over-the-counter acid-reflux drugs, that is.

The three of them would not believe me when I told them how I had purchased a medication that started foaming in your mouth as you ingested it, giving you the feeling of having your throat coated in cement.

"It couldn't be that bad," Maggie said.

"I tell you, I almost threw up at my desk," I said. "It was the most disgusting feeling ever."

Wanting to prove my point, I went to the bathroom and came back with three caplets.

"Go ahead," I coaxed. "Everybody's doing it."

They took my challenge and each popped a pill into their mouths.

"Start chewing!" I commanded, knowing what would soon be happening in their mouths.

Soon their faces all contorted and they started making gagging sounds.

"I can't breathe," Jen whispered.

"Water, water," Jaclyn begged.

Attempting to ram the foam farther down their throats, they kept chewing and swallowing while holding their hands in front of their faces to suppress their gag reflexes.

Enjoying this far too much, I pulled out my camera and started snapping away at them miming their death throes.

"Not too bad, is it?" I teased. "Anybody for another?"

After they all ran to the kitchen to get glasses of water, they were silent.

"Okay," they said, "we believe you."

After this torture, we thought it was time for a treat, so I ripped open a bag of chips and put *The Lost Boys* on. I had never seen the film but rented it on Jen's suggestion, as it had kept her up all night at a third-grade sleepover.

Jen watched half of it with her hands over her eyes, but the rest of us didn't find it all that scary. The most frightening thing about it was that Corey Haim managed to slip a pair of shoulder pads into every silk shirt and floor-length pastel jacket he wore.

Michael, Corey's brother in the film, played by a handsome young Jason Patric, was a terrible role model to kids in the area of peer pressure. In one scene, he literally jumped off a bridge because his friends did. While we watched the film, my three guests entertained me with stories from their childhood sleepovers.

"We did a lot of dance routines. Anything to stay awake. You NEVER wanted to go to sleep first," Jaclyn said. "If you did, people did things to you."

"Once we put a girl's hand into a bowl of water," Maggie said. "She totally peed herself. It was terrible."

"There's also always a point in the sleepover," Jaclyn said, "where you just want to leave."

What was she hinting at? Perhaps I needed to refill the chip bowl. Surely she couldn't be insinuating that sleeping on my floor was not going to be as comfortable as being at home, sleeping on her pillow-top mattress?

"If everybody was afraid to fall asleep or always wanted to leave the sleepovers at one point, why did anybody go?" I asked.

As I looked at them all sprawled out across my living room, wearing their pajamas, I realized that some things were definitely best experienced as a kid. We weren't going to egg a house, talk about our crushes, or put someone's hand in water while they slept, causing them to pee and leaving me to sop up a mess from my white rug, so I thought I would let them off the hook.

The point of a sleepover is togetherness, fun, and feeling

like you are definitely a part of something. When you are an adult and have friends so willing to participate in idiotic activities just to let you have the experience, you are a part of something great.

We were all asleep by 2 A.M. In our respective beds.

After I cleaned up the nacho-chip crumbs the next day, I started firing off e-mails to people to set up informational meetings on TV writing. After so many years behind the scenes, I had contacts but no real experience, though I had done some work in my postgrad class.

Unlike New York, where you had to send e-mails three times, everybody I wrote to got back to me right away and was willing to impart their wisdom.

Hannah insisted I meet her friend Vera, who was also Indian and was producing her own tween comedy about life for an Indian teenager.

"The family on the show is the best possible version of my family," she told me.

"Didn't your parents mind you making characters out of them?" I asked, imagining my parents' reaction.

"It took them a year to get used to it but they did," she said. "But then it took them years to get used to the fact that I was working in television. They kept telling me to go back to school to get a teaching degree as a backup."

Vera told me that she too spent her summers watching TV while growing up. I laughed when she told me her favorite shows. "I used to watch *Three's Company* and *Love Boat* every day," she said. Something about an apartment complex in

Santa Monica and comedy on the high seas must have really appealed to Indians in the eighties.

I asked Vera what prompted her to create her show, and she paused.

"Growing up in the eighties and nineties, I never saw anybody on TV that looked like me, except for Apu from *The Simpsons*. I wanted kids to see people who looked like them."

Vera generously gave me a list of books I should read, then e-mailed me later in the day with a list of websites I should check out and an offer for any further help I needed.

Everyone was so generous that it made the task ahead seem a little less arduous. But I didn't let myself forget that it would be a hard road. The year was coming to a close. I set out wanting to try a few lessons and now I found myself wanting to pursue a part in the most coveted industry around and relocate to a country famous for showing foreigners the door. It was like the difference between setting off to hike up a hilly trail and finding yourself at the foot of the Andes.

But before I could fully commit to this new mountain to climb, I had to tie up some loose ends with my original goals. Did I really have time to have a dog? This is a question dog owners don't seem to ask themselves enough. I wanted a dog, but whether I had the time and energy to give the dog what it wanted was questionable. Perhaps I was a better dog sitter than owner at this point. For the five years before this year, I had a life that was settled and ready to "insert dog here." No doubt a couple of years from now I would be back in that same position. But for this crazy year, I had to think about me and only me.

Did I really need to go to Disney World? That one was a no-brainer. Yes, I really, really needed to go.

→ TWENTY-SIX ←

the wonderful world of disney

When we were younger, every single Sunday night my sisters and I would eat *roti* and then settle in front of the television for the 6 P.M. Disney hour. We would beg our dad to tape us some of the programs, and viewed *Mickey and the Beanstalk* a dozen times. The tape of our favorite program, in which the characters do music videos, was almost worn out. For the longest time, I thought it was a female chipmunk that sang "Dress You Up in My Love," not Madonna. We later taped shows for Sumeet, who could not get enough of watching *Lambert*. When he was five, I was in my first year of college and came back at Christmas with something he had always wanted: a pair of Mickey Mouse ears. I had just bought them at the mall, but now that I was going to Disney World, I could finally get an authentic pair.

I had extended the invitation to all my siblings to join in on the trip. I contemplated extending it to my parents, but missing out on Disney World had never been a major regret of theirs, and we knew they would not go on a single ride. As the months passed, everybody's schedule became more hectic until only Navroop was left. I was disappointed that we couldn't all go together, but the list of places we had never been was astronomically long, so no doubt we would be able to have another voyage of mutual discovery sometime in the future.

Navroop and I headed to Orlando the second week of December, after she had completed her master's degree. I was finally going to see Disney World. After a childhood of watching our televised Disney cartoons, we were going to get to experience the mythical place that our schoolmates used to tell us about after every summer vacation.

The second we stepped off the plane, I felt stifling in my sweats tucked into my boots. My winter coat itched as it rested on my arm, heated by the thick Florida air. We made our way to the unsurprisingly named Magic Express, a convenient free bus that shuttled us to the hotel. I watched anxiously out the window as the sun started descending. By the time the bus dropped off all of the passengers, it was dusky, but the residual vitamin D floating in the air triggered the pleasure centers in my brain.

"Can you feel the heat?" I asked Navroop.

"I sure can," she answered, pushing back the nest of baby hair that always tormented her on humid days.

We checked in and I immediately changed into sandals and a T-shirt so we could go out exploring. As we were staying at a Disney resort, we were eligible for their complimentary transportation around the theme parks. It was 8 P.M., so we were advised that the only thing we could properly see in a couple of hours was downtown Disney.

"Sounds good," we said, imagining a swinging downtown center where the characters went to unwind after a long day marching in parades and taking photos with crying toddlers. I wondered if Mickey drank a tumbler of scotch before bed. Donald struck me as a real partier, but no doubt Goofy turned down their many requests to "hit downtown" in favor of going home to his family. I base this on nothing but the characters' performances in *Mickey and the Beanstalk*.

Disney World is a magical wonderland. In fact, that description would be highly endorsed by the Disney Corporation, as *magical* is their magic word. Everywhere we went, we were told to "have a magical day" or "a magical meal." The phone operator wished us a "magical evening" and a buffet attendant described the custard tart from a dessert table as "a magical experience."

"Let's not stay too late, though," I told Navroop. "I really want to swim tonight in that pool."

She rolled her eyes and nodded. When we were exploring the hotel grounds, I discovered a small and completely secluded little pool in the courtyard directly behind our room. It had no deep end, rendering it virtually impossible for me to drown. I had packed my whole swimming kit and pledged to get in that pool and practice swimming.

I had mentioned this to Navroop more times than I had realized.

"Dear God, I get it," she said. "You want to go to the pool. We'll make sure you go to the pool. You're like a little baby."

After a fifteen-minute bus ride, we were downtown. My vision of downtown failed to take into consideration that Disney is created for family enjoyment. Instead of the casino and dance club I expected to find, it was wall-to-wall stores, a movie theater just in case hours of rides and attractions didn't entertain you enough, and a row of restaurants.

As it was almost Christmas, the stores were jammed with Disney-themed ornaments that did make it look quite fun to have a tree on which to place your glitter-covered Tinker Bell. We wandered around from store to store, where almost every living consumer product out there had been Disney-fied. There were Mickey-ears Rice Krispie Treats, *Aladdin* boxer shorts, *Cinderella* charm bracelets, *Pinocchio* glasses, and *Little Mermaid* toys and games.

Some stores were dedicated solely to one character, some solely to a certain category of merchandise. Whatever you wanted, Disney had it.

I imagined how we would have reacted here had our parents taken us when we were younger, and can admit it would have been mayhem. I recalled a woman on the New York subway berating her young son, saying, "Jeez, Norman. You're so single-minded. All you want are toys. It's so sad."

If she had remembered childhood, she would have realized that Norman was not alone in this desire. All kids want toys. All the time. That is the nature of being a kid. There is no understanding of money, and it's not that they are materialistic. It is that toys are shiny, sparkly, exciting, and enticing.

When I was seven, my parents took us to the science center and my dad said we could all pick out one thing from the gift shop. My sisters all chose little toys and trinkets, but I chose a solid wood jewelry box with a maple leaf on the center of the lid. I had to have it. My dad pulled me aside and said, "That's expensive."

I nodded, thankful that he had filled me in on that fact, but wondered why he wasn't telling the shopkeeper to wrap it up.

"Do you like it that much?" he asked.

"Yes," I responded, having liked it for the past one minute and considering that a substantial period of time.

"Okay," he said. "Just don't tell your sisters."

When we got into the car, I wanted to play with everyone else's toys.

I now see how it would have been impossible for my parents to take us all to Disney. There were a lot of us, and after flights, accommodations, park entry for seven people, not to mention meals and the countless toys we would no doubt have cried for, it would never have made sense to people who paid for their cars in cash and sewed clothes for their daughters.

After multiple-scooped ice-cream cones and a tour of all of the greatest merchandise that Disney had ever made, we caught our bus back to the hotel, which, at ten-thirty, was dead silent.

"Okay," I said to Navroop. "It's time."

It was more than eighty degrees still and one of the things I always dreamed of when I couldn't swim was a dip in a pool on a warm night. Changing giddily into my bathing suit, I grabbed a handful of towels from the counter and headed out the door.

"Oh," I said. "I just realized I won't be able to see anything once I take off my glasses. You're going to have to come with me."

"Oh, man." Navroop sighed, grabbing a magazine from her bag. "Let's go already."

"Are you sure you don't want to swim, too?" I asked her. "I brought two bathing suits."

"No thanks," she said. "You know I can't swim."

I offered to teach her, but in the end we both agreed that my eight hours of tenure in the pool would not be of much assistance to another beginner.

The pool was completely empty when we arrived. Navroop made herself comfortable on one of the chaise longues while I handed her my glasses and groped my way over to the pool.

The water was warm. I glided onto my back and looked up, gazing at the stars I rarely saw in the city.

"Do you want me to show you my swimming skills?" I asked Navroop.

"Okay," she said in a tone that conveyed a desire for rain to begin.

"Just let me get warmed up here," I said.

After a warm-up that was longer in minutes than the pool was in feet, I put my head under the water, pushed off the edge, and began the art of swimming.

"Refreshing!" I exclaimed as I wiped the water from my eyes.

"You splash a lot," Navroop said. "Are you supposed to splash that much?"

"Oh, what do you know?" I snapped, going back to the serenity of floating on my back. For the next half hour I practiced swimming in exactly four strokes. Right arm forward, left arm forward, right hand forward, head out to breathe and sputter. Then I would stand up and heave in ten breaths and start again. The water and I were going to have to build up our mutual trust, hopefully without the aid of "trust falls" at a corporate retreat. But I was willing to keep going.

The next day we woke up bright and early and walked over to the Epcot Center. As it was the middle of the week, and kids were still in school, the lines were manageable. In three hours, we traveled across the world, taking a jaunty boat cruise through Mexico and a more treacherous cruise through Scandinavian history, and watching Asian acrobats. I stood in line to get a photo with a princess and wandered over to the area designated for Canada, hoping to find some *poutine* but instead only finding large nightshirts with photos of grizzly bears on them and cutesy sayings like "I'm Beary Tired!"

For lunch we headed back to our hotel, which was situated on a makeshift boardwalk. Ferries would pull up to transport you to the adjacent hotel, fifty feet away. The boardwalk was littered with seniors in motorized scooters, zipping along at a steady clip of 5 mph. One of the hotels had a fake beach that led to water you were not allowed to swim in, which was just as well, as somehow a pirate ship had become marooned on the sand. We treated our stomachs to a greasy, heavy meal to ready them for the rides we were going to hit at Hollywood Studios.

The studios were easily accessed from the ferries, which

we had ridden the night before just for fun. When the captain, dressed in his nautical white culottes, mentioned the studios in his audio tour of the area, he said that they were "just a short walk of about a mile." The crowd's gasps made it obvious that they would be frequenting the ferry system for the duration of their stay.

We walked over, on a lovely trail beside a little creek. At one point I looked down and a tiny little bunny was sitting quietly beside the path.

"Do you think Disney put that there to make this a 'magical' walk?" Navroop asked. We weren't sure. We were changing hotels that day, but the hotels kindly sent our luggage over so we could check in later; with this taken care of, we were able to plot out a full afternoon of amusement.

The first order of business was hitting the rides with the greatest nausea factor. Gills don't scream on rides. We are not those people with their arms up and smiles on their faces. We are the ones who look as if an assassin is choking them from behind and simultaneously pushing on their bladders. After two rides of plunging and one roller coaster where Navroop and I both reached out to grab each other's arms, not as a sign of solidarity but more as a declaration of if-I-die-on-this-you're-coming-down-with-me, we decided to give our stomachs a rest.

It's in the territory of the calmer rides that you encounter the children. Pardon me, the princesses. Every other girl under the age of ten was dressed as one of the Disney heroines. Belle from *Beauty and the Beast* seemed to be the reigning queen. That made me happy, because any story that extols the beauty of a really hairy paramour is tops in my book. Besides Belles, there were plenty of Minnie Mouses, Princess Jasmines, Pocahontases, and some generic haphazard princess outfits that parents had obviously slapped together themselves.

I had a list of the classic rides I had to visit, so we made our way over to the *Star Wars* flight simulator. Standing in line with mainly five-to-eight-year-old boys and their parental guardians, we smiled when a boy said to his mother, "I hope the pilot stays on course this time," not realizing that the pilot would veer off course this and every other time he boarded the flight to Alderaan.

When the robot usher's voice alerted us that the flight was leaving, we all scrambled to our seats. A boy with his face painted like a tiger's sat behind me at the edge of his seat.

"When do we take off?" he asked his father impatiently.

"Oh my," said the woman on the other side of him, who seemed to be trying to help create an air of danger.

"We don't have a captain. Whoever will be our captain?"

The boy thought for a minute before responding, "Whoever is the biggest."

What classic kid logic. I recall having that mind-set myself when I was a child, that whoever was a year older or two inches taller was the unofficial leader of us.

When we exited our rocket ship, the sky was looking ominous, so we ducked into the safety of the Hall of Presidents. I admit I don't know the names of all of the U.S. presidents, but I let myself off the hook, as studies show most Americans don't either. Luckily a twenty-minute animatronics presentation was going to give us our historical education.

I was worried that as a show of patriotism, some guys in

the audience would pull out their muskets and offer a three-gun salute, but the beautiful emotional sentiment of the history of the world's superpower was jarringly interrupted when a voice boomed over the loudspeaker, "We said NO flash photography!" He didn't sound like he wanted us to have a magical experience.

After several more hours of rides and shows, we jumped onto the bus that was heading to our new resort. The first resort had been quiet and white-duveted, exactly what I wanted as an adult, but for our second night, I chose a hotel that I would have wanted to stay in as a child.

The hotel was African-themed and boasted its own wildlife reserve. If fifteen hours of shows, parades, Dumbo rides, and photos with Aladdin were not enough to entertain a family, they could return to the hotel and watch zebras and giraffes frolicking in their native habitat—a hotel courtyard.

Starved from our day of sightseeing, we put our names on the reservation list for the hotel's impressive-looking buffet and were nearly salivating on the floor when they called us for a table. Well schooled by the competitiveness of Indian wedding buffets, where aunties will elbow you to get another piece of chicken tikka masala, we bolted right for the line before our waiter even had time to take our drink order.

"Mmm, it all smells good," Navroop said, wafting in the aromas from the various meat slabs. Navroop had recently returned to eating meat after ten years as a devout vegetarian and was determined to make up for lost time.

I was so hungry that I grabbed a plate and actually jumped ahead of the first station to butt into line at a less trafficked area. "Oh, sorry," I said to my fellow buffeters, as if I didn't realize how the system worked. Layering veggies over couscous over salad over soup bowls over a plate of side dishes, I made my way back to the table.

The couple beside us was eating their dessert in utter silence. The man, who wore a button saying "It's My Birthday," had a plate laden with pastries and a napkin full of cookies for the road.

"Don't you love this soup?" I asked Navroop as I scraped my spoon vigorously around the bowl.

"It's delicious," she said. "Did you try the roast beef? It's so tender."

"Oh yes," I said. "It's great. But I think I like the couscous the best."

"Barry?" said the woman beside us to the birthday boy. "Could I have a cookie?"

Barry reluctantly slid the napkin over and they nibbled cookies in silence, both staring off into the distance. I wanted to take a photo of them and put it up on my fridge to remind myself of the realities of marriage whenever I daydreamed of my future husband.

"Round two?" Navroop asked. We both went back up to the buffet, our eyes darting back and forth between the buffet selection and our plates to make the best plan to maximize the capacity of the plate.

Back at our table, we moved around the water glasses and saltshakers to allow enough room for our toppling plates.

"This is just what I need," I said. "The one thing I don't like about traveling is that you always end up eating more fast food than you want. It's nice to have fresh food."

Barry didn't agree. When the bill arrived, he took a look

at it and shook his head, even though the per-person price is a flat rate that's written on the wall, and the drinks are free.

His wife looked uncomfortable as Barry reached for his wallet. "I just think," Barry said, "that for this price, there could be more of a selection."

Navroop and I looked at each other and made silent eyes; nonverbal gossiping is a skill Indians could trademark. More food for us, our eyes whispered.

We had saved the biggest for last. The next day we woke up early and prepared ourselves for the ultimate in magical experiences: the Magic Kingdom. When we were kids, it was the ads showing the Magic Kingdom that were particularly effective marketing on us. The castle looked enchanting. We longed to ride on the Dumbo ride and make terrified faces on Space Mountain. When I was in kindergarten, one of my favorite toys was a plastic radio that played an instrumental version of "It's a Small World After All," and when I saw the actual attraction in a commercial, I wanted desperately to be riding in that little boat through a cave of international wonders.

Arriving on Main Street USA, we didn't know where to begin. I was more than a little tempted to make my way over to the Bibbidi Bobbidi Boutique and have my hair princess-styled, but I knew it would likely take them three beauticians and multiple hours to fashion my hair into any semblance of a royal style.

We could see Dumbo swirling off in the distance, so made our way over to the ride. As expected, a number of Belles were in the line, but the costume prize of the day had to go to a preschool-age boy in a full Buzz Lightyear costume. The best part of the costume was that it had obviously been made at home. He wore all white, including tights that looked to be from a jazz-dance recital, and had strapped a surprisingly authentic-looking jet pack to his back.

"Hi there, little pilot," the ride attendant greeted him. "Would you mind taking off your helmet for the ride?"

Buzz nodded and climbed aboard a Dumbo with what was likely his long-suffering-at-the-sewing-machine mother. Navroop and I ran to the other side to find our own Dumbo, then wondered if two grown women could really fit into one tiny circus elephant together. Squeezing ourselves in, we pushed the lever to ascend higher and surveyed the rest of the kingdom.

"Let's do the ghost house next," Navroop said.

The ghost house featured a dark anteroom before you lined up for the ride. We could barely hear the spooky ghost sounds over the voices of the parents who were reassuring their children.

"Don't worry, Sean," one woman said. "It's just all make-believe. And look, there's another little boy up there."

Sean was not convinced, but his mother was not about to leave after waiting in line twenty minutes, so Sean was getting haunted whether he wanted to or not.

A toddler Minnie Mouse behind us pressed her face into her father's chest and shook her head.

"Don't worry," her father said. "Just keep your eyes closed the whole time." The father was holding Minnie as well as the hand of another little boy, so getting onto the ride looked as if it could be a more frightening experience for that family than the ride itself.

The ride attendant motioned to a specific cart and then you had approximately ten seconds to step onto a moving sidewalk and jump onto said cart before it disappeared into the darkness.

"Run for it," the father instructed his young son, hurling his son, daughter, and himself toward their cart.

The father and Minnie jumped on and the little boy just made it, an extra hoist from his father securing his footing.

There were at least ten motorized scooters parked outside the ride's entrance, making me wonder how somebody with limited mobility would suddenly have the lightness of foot to hurl themselves into a moving vehicle, but grandma after grandpa seemed to find their way onto a cart.

After hurtling through space on Space Mountain and spinning wildly on the teacups, we paused for a couple of mandatory parades before heading back to Hollywood Studios. At Navroop's insistence, we were going to the megashow *Fantasmic,* a pyrotechnic extravaganza where Mickey must escape the clutches of a selection of Disney's most wicked villains.

"Hurry up," Navroop said. "We're not going to get a seat."

The stadium could have easily held a thousand people, but Navroop did not want to leave it to chance. We ended up finding seats in the "Jafar" section and hoped nobody mistook us for costumed extras.

The show was as grandiose as expected, but the most spectacular thing about it was that every other person there was viewing it through the lens of their digital camera. This was an occurrence I noticed more and more at live events. Why enjoy the moment at the time when you can tape it and watch it at a subpar quality later?

But in this case, I did see the relevance. If you had carted your family of five from France or Nebraska and wandered around after your kids for five days while they rode every ride, you would want to record every moment. The second they forgot the fun they had and begged to return, you could pull out the tapes and let them relive it from the comfort of your living room.

As much as I was having a great time at Disney World, being there made me see that I would only want to return with kids of my own. And I still wish I had gone there as a kid myself. Magical experiences are most effective for people who still believe in magic, not those who are trying to get a spark back into their aimless lives.

In being honest with myself, I had to admit that part of my motivation for this year of adventures was not just to do all of the things I hadn't done when I was a kid. It was because I hadn't done any of the things I thought I would do as an adult.

I was thirty-one years old, and while everybody around me was getting married, buying homes, and having kids they would soon sign up for lessons and take to amusement parks, I was nowhere close to achieving any of it and I wanted it. But I wasn't going to find a husband or save the funds to buy a home in a year. I wondered sometimes, on days when I would surround myself with sugary reassurances, if that was ever going to happen.

Deep down, I knew it would, but at times, a lot of it felt

largely out of my control. And on the off chance that those things weren't going to happen for me, I had to feel as if I had some semblance of control over my own life. And in ways, I thought that correcting the past would somehow alter my DNA to make me the adult I wanted to be.

→ TWENTY-SEVEN ←

holiday special

Right before the holidays, my hometown friends and I gathered at Johanna's house. It was at her bachelorette weekend over a year ago that I had decided to set out on my quest, and now, at the end of it, I was at a surprise baby shower for her. She was due on Christmas Day and her giant belly swelled out from her tiny body.

"Do you have a good nipple salve?" our friend Sarah asked her. Sarah was already on baby number two, so was the expert of the group. I would have never believed as we sat around the school cafeteria table twelve years ago that one day we would be discussing nipple salves. But here we were, eating baked goods, trading recipes, and generally acting like civilized grown women.

Melodie was also hugely pregnant and due in February, so

there was a lot of impending excitement for the group. I was bursting because I knew of another piece of incredibly exciting news, but Jill, the friend whose secret I was sworn not to reveal, was taking her time and it was driving me crazy. "Come onnnnn," I said, making crazy eyes at her. Finally, she cracked and told everyone she was engaged. The year ahead was going to be a great one for everyone. I didn't know what next year held for me, but if it would be anything close to as life altering as this one had been for me, it would be something worth waiting for.

Although Christmas was fast approaching, I wasn't dying to go home for the holidays. When you don't believe in Jesus and are too old to believe in Santa, what necessity is there to go home? My family didn't put up a tree, our gift exchange was pared down each and every year, and our holiday dinner was usually supplied from a fast-food establishment. I would have been just as happy to sit in my apartment eating bag after bag of nacho chips while watching reruns of 227.

But guilt is a powerful motivator. My parents saw it as vacation time, thus offering no reason why we wouldn't come home. And people seemed to raise their eyebrows when I even mentioned sitting around alone instead of going home for holidays that we barely celebrated.

"Even if you don't celebrate," they would say, "don't you want to spend time with your family?"

Um . . . yes?

The foremost cause of stress for people in the holiday season is spending time with their family. I anticipated three days of reverting back to childhood behaviors. My sisters and I would sit in the basement, eat junk food, watch movies, play

Scrabble, and make many, many jokes, mostly at the expense of one another. In our house, there was no turkey dinner to devour or cashmere sweater waiting for me under the tree, so the normally motivating factors of gifts and gluttony had no pull. But this year, going home for the holidays did have one major selling point.

Auggie would be there. Auggie had become our new bag of chips. We all wanted our equal share. He gave me my fill of canine fun. He wasn't my dog, yet I wanted him around all the time. "I'm going to the library," I would call Gurpreet and say, as I was already walking over. "I will pop by on the way in." When I got there, I would run around so Auggie could chase me, and throw him his ball. He would sit at my feet and I would stroke his long teddy-bearish hair, then reluctantly leave when I noticed the time.

When we would meet at the shopping center equidistant from both of our apartments, he would pull the leash out of Gurpreet's hand and come tearing toward me. When I took him to the dog park, I stood proudly while everybody showered me with compliments on his cuteness, then giggled every time he ran after a ratty tennis ball, as if he was the only dog with that ability. I got the perfect amount of canine interaction being a dog aunt, so for the time being, I decided to put my own plans of dog ownership aside. I would likely waver on this decision each day of the coming year, but with new goals in mind that could leave my life up in the air for the foreseeable future, I didn't want to take a poor pet along for the ride.

When Navjit asked if Auggie could come home early for the holidays, Gurpreet knew she had to oblige. Navjit had made the exciting decision to go along with Navroop when she moved to New Zealand. They were leaving in two weeks, so this was possibly the last Christmas we would all spend together for a long time. Most important to Navroop and Navjit was that they wouldn't see Auggie for a long time.

My mom brought out a bag one night and presented us all with our gifts. We all got a plain long-sleeved shirt. For Navroop, she also bought a cookbook with instructions on how to make exciting incarnations of Navroop's favorite food, cupcakes. She called Auggie over and presented him with his gifts, a multicolored ball and a Christmas place mat on which we could put his dog bowls in the front hall. We giggled to one another when we saw him run away with the ball in his mouth. No matter how many times my mom yelled, "He needs to go to the washroom. Someone take him to the washroom!" in the hope of sparing her carpets, it was obvious that she loved her furry new family member. This love may have also been due to the fact that he followed her around everywhere she went and would bark at my dad to leave the family room every night so he, Auggie, could watch the 11 P.M. news alone with my mom. That was her favorite trick.

My parents actually wanted to hear about New York. Unlike eight years ago, when they thought it was the land of muggers and street gangs, they now liked to hear about the city. They wanted to hear about my apartment and oohed and aahed when I told them the appliances were stainless steel.

"You can come to visit when I go back," I told my mom. She agreed. Though I already anticipated a New York visit filled with arguments and sideways glances at suspicious-looking hobos, I wanted to have an apartment that my parents would see was nice, and a life that they would see I had done well in, and feel proud that I was living a good life.

Most important, I wanted them to accept me and whatever choices I made in my life, rather than push on me the ones they wanted.

When my dad was growing up, my grandparents saved every dime they had to give him the money to go to college. They didn't get to be educated, but they saw the potential in him and wanted to nurture it, knowing it would pay off. Because of their sacrifice, my dad was able to move to Canada and sponsor his whole family to join him. Because of this, instead of toiling away on the farm, making *roti* for a family of ten every night, my grandmother rode a plane for the first time in her life, saw snow for the first time in her life, and still got to go back to India when she desired, holding court in her courtyard as her old friends came to see her and hear tales of her new life.

When my dad was in college, he saw an advertisement for a car that he thought was the picture of American luxury: the Chevrolet Impala. "I told myself, one day I will drive that car," he said. It was a giant box of a car, nothing glamorous or exciting, but he bought himself one and carted us around in it during our childhoods, feeling like the picture of success. He and my mom, like my grandparents before them, saved their money to give us the opportunities that they never had themselves. My grandmother never thought she would see the mythical land of Canada and my mom never thought she would see the famous city known as New York, and I didn't want to leave that wish unfulfilled.

I had been unabashedly selfish for a year, pursuing the

childhood I had always wanted, having wished my parents had done right by me. Growing up, I always wished they could have been more supportive, they could have been more understanding, and they could have said "I love you" just once. But now I knew that they did what they could and that it was time I did right by them, as they had neither the childhoods nor adulthoods that they had wanted for themselves.

Mostly, though, I had a desire to keep doing right by myself. "You look so happy," people would remark to me after I left my job and moved away. I looked happy because I actually was. I had a life that allowed me a brief pause to live a dream, and I had people who went above and beyond to keep my head dreamily floating in the clouds that whole time.

I'd felt fairly unsupported in my desires as a kid. As an adult, I had more support in my life than most people. From encouragement from strangers in Speedos, interest in my next activity from colleagues, friends and family who offered everything from dog loaners and driving lessons to tennis partners and travel companions, it was taking a village to make my childhood a reality and I had to keep going forward.

If I have kids, I can only hope that one day, after they finish with the child beauty-pageant circuit I force them into, they will look upon their lives and feel that they are fulfilling and full. I will tell them stories of their great-grandmother watching soap operas, and when they ask me why grandma keeps making them clean the house on their visits, I will tell them the tale of two young people who left India to make brighter futures for themselves.

"Did they really not have electricity?" the kids will ask.

"Yes," I will say. "And their whole house was smaller than

your basement playroom. Now let's go over the Punjabi alphabet again before you forget."

They will travel, they will take lessons, and when we sit down to dinner together every night, silence will never be allowed. We will talk about our hopes and dreams and be a team whose members are there for one another. And our family motto will be to never, ever stop pursuing the lives we want, no matter what.

That is the vision I have for the future, but getting there means continuing to have years that build upon this one. With the new year fast approaching, I knew I had to keep motivated. My greatest fear was to have this amazing, eye-opening year and then slip back into my former life the next year. I could see myself walking to work in my long down jacket, stopping for my morning croissant, sending out and reading hundreds of e-mails, and jonesing for my afternoon chocolate pick-me-up. I wanted to avoid that at all cost. If it somehow happened, it couldn't be because I had just given up when the calendar struck December 31.

My Christmas gift to myself was booking a trip to L.A. I was going to finally go to L.A., call every Tom, Dick, and Harry in town, and hope that somebody, anybody would meet with me. If not, perhaps it was the harsh lesson in the competitiveness and difficulty of the business that I needed to learn.

I didn't delude myself into thinking I would sit down and write the most brilliant television work the industry had ever seen and be instantly feted and ushered into jobs on all of my favorite shows. But a year ago I also didn't think I would learn to swim, or leave my job, or walk down Main Street USA. Life was becoming a day-by-day adventure, and who knew what would be next? There was so much more to do. So please disregard the line after this one, because dear reader, I hope this is just the beginning.

The end.

ACKNOWLEDGMENTS

A million thank-yous to the wonderful and talented Sarah Stein, and the amazing team at Riverhead for believing in this book. And for believing in me well before there was a reason to do so, thank you to Agent/Asian Extraordinaire Sam Hiyate.

Thanks to Elizabeth Kribs, Trena White, Ashley Dunn, Doug Pepper, and everyone on my home team at McClelland & Stewart, peer readers and all-around good ladies Madeleine Di Gangi, Jaclyn Atwood and Jennifer Knox, the Gilda's Club staff and campers, Angela Saclamacis at Disney, Ryan Wagman for the book's title, Michael McGrath for basically everything, my sisters for their fact-checking and general love and encouragement, everyone who is featured in and has supported this book, and a debt of gratitude to Hannah Sung, without whom I would have never written this book or likely, anything at all.

ABOUT THE AUTHOR

Rupinder Gill's writing has been published in the *National Post* and on the *McSweeney's* website. She has written for CBC Radio and Canada's *This Hour Has 22 Minutes*.